Ten Simple Steps

for success in sales

Life-changing advice from Britain's leading salesman
John T Cross

First published in Great Britain by Pen Press

All paper used in the printing of this book has been made from wood
grown in managed, sustainable forests.

ISBN13: 978-1-78003-341-9

Printed and bound in the UK
Pen Press is an imprint of
Indepenpress Publishing Limited
25 Eastern Place
Brighton
BN2 1GJ

A catalogue record of this book is available from
the British Library

I dedicate this book to my darling wife Sherry, who has always supported me in everything I have ever done and helped build the foundation on which my life has been based.

Introduction

One of my favourite pastimes as a young child was watching my father work. He was a butcher and the family lived in a modest flat above his shop. I can vividly remember standing at the window, the curtain curled around me, motionless and completely absorbed as I watched my father below in the yard making sausages. I had done this often since about the time I had learned to walk.

Looking down from my secret vantage point above, I could see the top of his head and his strong hands working efficiently and without hesitation. He'd be standing by a giant hopper, rhythmically taking the meat fed out from the machine, twisting it into a four-sausage link and placing it into a pile. Feed, twist, pile. Feed, twist, pile. Feed, twist, pile. Again and again. The sight was utterly hypnotic and the finished sausages just kept piling up.

It was not until some years later that I discovered that, in fact, one part of this industrious scenario was missing. It emerged that my uncle Gordon was concealed further away in the yard, out of my line of sight, repeatedly filling up the machine with the raw ingredients that went into making the sausages.

I now believe that discovering that missing piece of the jigsaw was a revelation that helped change the course of my whole life. In a flash, I understood that it was only by Gordon's actions keeping the hopper full that the whole process worked and my father was able to make his ever-growing pile of sausages. To me, this was a salutary lesson indeed.

Even though I was very young, I had, by the time of this revelation, already decided I was destined for a career in sales. Although 'destined' is perhaps the wrong word. To be more accurate, I was passionate about pursuing a career in sales, which is probably why in my hunger to get started I saw everything as a lesson which could help me in my choice of career.

After discovering my uncle's role, I surmised that the hopper represented a salesperson's portfolio of contacts, both prospects and suspects. The former being most likely to buy and the latter those 'definite maybes' that other salespeople seem prepared to wait around for, for months if not years, instead of getting out there and finding better prospects. You know, the sort of salespeople who spend their career pining over the ones who once expressed a tentative interest and may eventually say yes (but probably never will).

To my way of thinking, if I kept my imaginary hopper constantly full of prospects, with an impressive flow of new ones always coming in, then an impressive flow of signed-up, paying clients would naturally ensue. What could be simpler? All I had to do was set my mind to constantly filling the hopper and success was assured. It is simply a numbers game.

So that is what I have done throughout my sales career and I do think that understanding this simple, yet vital, fact has greatly contributed to my success. I have been lucky enough to have had an enormously rewarding time in this industry and along the way have won a great many awards and commendations for my sales techniques. As my career has progressed, I have been asked by many of my colleagues in the industry to share some of my sales secrets to help them in their own endeavours. Now, at last, this is what I have done and *Ten simple steps for success in sales* is the result of what I have learned over the past 50 years out on the road in this green and pleasant land.

Success in sales is not rocket science. There are no complex formulas that will lead to guaranteed success. To me it is all about a mix of certain key skills, some hard work and cultivating some important personal values such as honesty, trustworthiness and faith.

In *Ten simple steps for success in sales*, I have broken down these essentials into ten steps, each one illustrating a different route to sales success in a lively and practical way. Each one of these tried and tested techniques can work in isolation and you would almost certainly see an improvement in your sales statistics if you followed just one of them. Do them all at the same time, though, and your sales figures will go through the roof.

This book will show you how to:

- Build rapport and trust
- Listen to clients and handle objections from the toughest prospects
- Build stronger customer relationships
- Gain superior insight into both your product and your industry – and use this knowledge
- Motivate yourself, even when times are tough
- Keep your foot on the accelerator all the time and constantly exceed your targets
- And stop complacency and arrogance in its tracks.

Some of the elements, such as 'work hard', or 'learn everything you can about your product', or 'be honest', may seem completely obvious on first reading. I already do that, you might think. Except you probably don't. Hand on heart, can you honestly say you always follow leads through? Are always good to your word? Do you always put every effort into going the extra mile? If you do, you are certainly the exception.

In my experience, salespeople rarely follow through on their initial approaches. All too often they get distracted by definite maybes and even sometimes miss obvious buying signals from their prospects. Indeed, most of the salespeople I have come across in my years on the road are simply not trying hard enough. The result? They don't make nearly as much income as they imagined they would.

Time and again, these less-than-successful salespeople have turned to me and said, 'John, you are lucky that you have always been so successful.'

Let me tell you, luck has nothing to do with it. I have never been afraid of hard work and will always, always go the extra mile. I am never content to be just 'good' at something. I always want to be the best. When I hit my targets, I don't switch off and think, well, that is that, it is time to take my foot off the accelerator. I set new targets. I see how far I can really go. There is no limit to my horizons.

Anyone can be a good salesperson. I was not born a good salesperson. I had no real advantages. I lived in a council house in Leicester for most of my childhood. But, from the start, I made the most of the qualities I had. I was good at debating and could think fast on my feet. Plus, when a chance was presented to me, I didn't ever hesitate to grab it and hold on.

My earliest memory of this is when I got a second chance to get into grammar school, having failed my 11 Plus. Failing that important exam was enough of a jolt to the system to make me study very hard and do all I could to get the 13 Plus. I managed, through hard work and sheer force of will, to pass the 13 Plus, and then the only thing standing in my way was the interview to get into the grammar school I wanted. My dad came along with me because the whole family recognised that it was going to be one of the most important days of my life. We got there with time to spare and had a wander around to keep me calm and walk off the nerves. One of the buildings we passed on this walk was the Leicester College for Arts and Technology and I remember glancing up at it as I walked by with my tummy full of butterflies. Half an hour later, right smack bang in the middle of the interview, the headmaster of this grammar school stopped and said, 'Tell me, John, what is that building over there?

'Leicester College of Arts and Technology,' I shot straight back, with a confident smile.

'How do you know?' he asked, looking impressed and returning my smile.

'I noticed it was written on the board when I walked past, Sir,' I said.

The headmaster turned triumphantly round to the deputy head and said, 'This is just the sort of boy we want in our school. John is observant. He sees the world around him and knows what is going on.'

I was offered a place at the grammar school and that, in turn, opened many doors for me. It gave me an edge, some polish and some useful skills at maths and English grammar. The experience also taught me some real life lessons. If you work hard and are straight, ethical and honest, another door will always open. Plus, if you have a twinkle in your eye and can think fast on your feet, things will usually work out just fine in the end.

I have learned many more lessons along the way and am always more than happy to share them. I fervently believe that everyone can learn the art of successful selling and that I can help them multiply their income manyfold if they simply follow the advice on these pages. How can I say this? Because I have been doing this for half a century, consistently reaching and exceeding my own goals and multiplying my income by many hundreds of percents using these self-same strategies and techniques.

Central to my successful sales formula is developing successful and fruitful long-term relationships with clients. 'Selling' does not just take place at the end of a transaction, when money changes hands. The process begins long before that final commitment and, if you handle it correctly, should go on a good long time after you've got the cheque in your hands. Long-term partnerships and repeat business, where both sides feel really good about working together, are the key to a successful and lucrative career in sales.

No one likes being 'sold to' and today's buyers are more sophisticated and knowledgeable than ever before. If they feel badgered or hectored, or that you are not on their side, rest assured that they will go elsewhere. No, the job of a modern salesman is to motivate your prospects into action. You won't ever do that unless you are truly in tune with what you are selling and have taken the time to properly understand your prospect's thoughts, desires and perceptions.

Ten simple steps for success in sales is a practical guide of how to do just this. It will show you how to build those relationships and how to deal with any reluctance on the part of the buyer. There are tips on how to qualify would-be clients and when the right time to walk away from time-wasters is. It is also a practical guide on how to order your own daily working schedule by setting meaningful goals and then why it is important to monitor them on a week-by-week basis. It shows the value of learning how to use your time more efficiently and sticking to what you are good at.

I confess that these methods are not all the product of my own trial and error, although many of them are. Over the years I have attended hundreds of sales conferences and heard dozens of the best salespeople in the world speak. I have heard many pearls of wisdom from people I respect and am not too proud to go out and try them for myself. I can honestly vouch that these pearls do work and I am more than happy to pass them on now that I have extensively 'road tested' them.

I know that the harder I work, the luckier I get. Success in sales is not about a quick push and then sitting back to see what happens. It is a way of life. *Ten simple steps for success in sales* shows that with a little extra effort, and the benefit of some simple tools, it is possible to become very lucky indeed. Whatever your starting point, or level of experience, you will get better at selling if you use the *Ten simple steps for success in sales*. I guarantee it.

Step One: Survive

I often tell people that I was depressed once. I remember the occasion well. It was three o'clock on a Tuesday afternoon and it lasted about one minute. That's it.

It has always been a source of constant amazement to me how many people are prepared to simply accept that things aren't going well. They reinforce the apparent misery of their hopeless situation by blaming it all on a run of luck, or an economic downturn, or some crisis or other. Indeed they blame anything but their own negative state of mind. I always ask people who act like this, why would you do that?

You will never be an effective salesperson until you learn the first golden rule: survive.

There is always a way to survive. It doesn't matter how hard your situation is, or how bleak the outside world appears to others; it is your perception of how things are that counts.

If you know how to survive you stand a much better chance of forging your way in the world and meeting all your ambitions. Look at it from the other side. Would you buy anything from someone who looked downtrodden, downbeat and, well, desperate? Of course not. You'd go to the guy with a smile on his face and a cheery disposition.

If a person hasn't got that survival skill you can see it a mile off. There is a look of despair in their eyes, their shoulders are hunched and their whole demeanour is one of complete failure.

We all have bad spells. It is not possible to always be successful day after day, but if you let something bring you down the bad spell will go on and on and on. It is up to you to change the bad spell into something good. It is that simple.

About 40 years ago, I was sales director of a plastics company and life seemed to be bumping along OK. Then, on Boxing Day, I got the letter that every employee dreads. It said that my services were no longer required because the company was being taken over. The company offered the bare minimum redundancy settlement, so as soon as the Christmas break was over I decided I had better pay a visit to the local labour office, as it was known back then. The very cheery young assistant offered her sympathies at my predicament and told me to return in a fortnight when they would begin paying me state benefits. She added that I had better not get my hopes up about finding employment any time soon because the job market was terrible. Indeed, she had hardly needed to say that. The country was blighted by miner's strikes and the three-day week. The broadsheet newspapers only had a handful of jobs advertised each day and none of them seemed suitable to my skills. It was then that it really hit me. Crikey, I thought to myself, I am on the dole. I have to say, as a proud man, this didn't suit me one bit.

Instead of collapsing into a pit of despair, I immediately sat down and thought: what can I do? I was very interested in music and thought: that is an industry I'd like to get into. Over the next few days I wrote out a letter and a CV, explaining who I was and why I thought I could be of use to a company in the hifi industry. I copied it more than 100 times and sent it to every company I could think of and then some more besides. Seven days later I had a phone call inviting me to Chiswick in west London for an interview for a job as marketing director of an international hifi stereo group. That interview was on a Thursday and by the Saturday I was in America, having taken the job and then been asked to go out there and see a supplier.

Some of my friends said to me, you lucky beggar. 'How did you manage to leave one job and get another great one straight away?' they asked.

It was not luck, I told them. My new job did not drop out of the clear blue sky. If you want to survive, there is no time to wallow in your own misery. Do what I did; write letters, get out there and put your name about. If you don't for one moment get felled by one blow in your career, you will always find something good around the corner.

Luck has nothing to do with it. What you do with your life is up to you and you alone. It is a question of choice. We all have a range of alternatives that we can choose. Every morning when we step out of the door we have options as to how we are going to face the day and deal with things. Problems will always come your way, they always do, but it is your choice how you deal with those problems and survive.

Positive mental attitude

In life, either you have a positive mental attitude (PMA), or you don't. I've been very fortunate that I have only ever suffered from PMA, but that doesn't mean I am *luckier* than the next man. It is simply how I judge the impact of the various situations that befall me.

Very early on in my married life with my darling wife Sherry, we lost our dear daughter Alison to viral pneumonia when she was aged just 16 months. She had been born with Down's syndrome and had been ill for some time beforehand. It was, of course, a devastating event for both Sherry and me. We had a choice, though, as to how we treated our loss. We could have, quite understandably, gone into meltdown and gone on asking, why us? Why her? Why now? Or we could take the experience and the short time we had with our beautiful daughter, and use it positively for the rest of our lives.

Sherry and I both took the second option and, I believe, we became better people because of what had happened to us. Sherry, for example, chose to throw her energies into bereavement counselling because she felt she could help other people thanks to what we had been through.

For me, the experience strengthened my faith in God and made me look at my belief more deeply. I realised that nothing is ever a waste and when someone like Alison comes along and dies young, it is not a wasted life. It was therapeutic to address it and, even now, we still talk about Alison on a daily basis, even though she died more than 30 years ago.

With the right PMA human beings can overcome the most dreadful situations. I was once fortunate enough to have an audience with a man who had been a prisoner of war in Vietnam for seven years, with most of that time spent in solitary confinement.

How do you survive in that situation? I asked. He explained that something called tap code, which you learn in the forces, had saved his life. In tap code, one tap means A, two B and so on. It's similar to Morse code. Now, the Vietnamese soon got on to this, because the Americans who were all kept in separate cells were all tapping messages to one another. So they manacled their hands so they couldn't do it. That meant that they had to find another way to try to communicate. So they coughed out the taps. Cough, then cough, cough, cough and so on. The Vietnamese got on to that too and gagged the soldiers. So they had to find another way and began kicking their cell walls to communicate. Of course, their captors got on to this too, and manacled the legs so they were completely immobile. They were kept like this for weeks at a time. But do you know what? He and his buddies never gave in. They knew they had to keep in touch and spent their whole time finding new and ingenious ways to do it. So, for example, when they were allowed out to clean the cells and sweep them, they used the rhythmic swishing of the broom as a tap. 'Swish swish, swish, swish swish swish, swish swish.' They did anything and everything to communicate and survive.

This chap also said that he had learned to play golf in the long hours alone inside his prison cell. He used to imagine the course at Georgia where he had previously played and went through each hole in his mind, from teeing off to putting the ball in the hole at the end. When he was finally released from his prison all those years later one of the first things he did, once he had recovered from his ordeal, was play a round of golf at the same golf course. He went all the way around and got in at 18 over. One of his friends said, 'That is phenomenal, you haven't played for ten years and you're on 18 over!'

'Hell,' he said. 'In my cell I was on three under.'

What an attitude! Who could fail to be inspired by someone like this?

Survival is all about the way you look at things. Everything comes down to making sure you survive and hang on in there. You have to have faith that you can do it and believe that you are following your destiny. Trust in yourself, because you will be amazed what you can do if you put your mind to it.

My advice to everyone is to view every experience positively, not negatively. Never let anything be a major hurdle that can bring you down on your hands and knees, never to rise again. That doesn't mean that you won't have some bad days. Of course you will. We all do. However, you just have to deal with it and move on. That is what life is all about, and in selling believing this is more important than anything, because if you can't do that you are dead in the water. You are trapped. Stuck where you are. If you let negativity take over you are never going to make any progress, or convince anyone that they should listen to your story.

I often say to myself: I am in total control of my life. Why would I allow circumstances or anything untoward dictate to me and change what I am going to do tomorrow, or next week? If you want to get to the top in sales, that is the attitude you have to have. You can't be affected by negative events and let things get to you. That doesn't mean that you don't learn from the bad times, or that you have to become inhuman. It means you always have to be prepared to pick yourself up, dust yourself down and go out the next day to see some fresh prospects.

Survival skills can be learned

Sir Winston Churchill was once invited to give a speech at Eton on prize-giving day. The great man stood up and said to the assembled crowd of schoolboys in his distinctive booming voice, 'Never, ever give in.' Then he sat back down. That was it. It was all he had to say. But it was all there in one sentence and he was absolutely right. If you are serious about survival, you never, ever give in.

You should always hang on in there and fight whenever there is a chance to hang on in there and fight. Yes, there will be times when survival is about hanging on by your fingernails and it can be painful. But you can always hang on by your fingernails for as long as it takes if you choose to do it.

The good news is that all of us are born with survival skills built right into our DNA. That is why we are still here. We have a history of survival, or the whole human race would have gone the way of the dinosaurs. Plus, anything we don't know about survival can be learned. I always think of it as being a bit like mountaineering. If someone really wants to climb Everest, they can learn the skills that, all things being equal, will help them survive climbing up that mountain and then come back down again. Whereas the odds are, if anyone attempts to go up Everest without first learning those skills, they probably won't survive and come home.

Learning how to survive a career in sales is far easier than learning how to climb the world's biggest mountain. At its simplest, it means getting up in the morning and putting on a big smile. Accompany it with a rousing mantra of, 'I canna, I musta, I willa,' and you are really off to the races. It is just a question of being positive and, believe me, if you say this mantra enough, you won't only believe it; you will live it.

I always, always choose to be positive, even with things that never usually work out well for me like exams. I hate exams and have failed more than I care to mention. But I never give up. I refuse to be negative. I just work harder, study more and enter any examination with a broad smile.

I didn't always know how to survive. I am quite happy to admit that I very nearly didn't get through my early days as a salesman. In fact, I would have got out of the industry altogether had it not been for the efforts of one man who kept me in the business by showing me how to survive. His name was Jim Wallinger and he was my manager at Hambro Life. I had had quite a good start at Hambro Life and a number of great breaks. In a very short space of time I had a clutch of plaques and awards which proclaimed that I was a great salesman. I put them up all over the walls and basked in the glory of my success. Unfortunately, I was so busy basking in my reflected glory that I forgot that I was actually supposed to go out there and sell something. As a result, my income plummeted and I was no longer the golden boy. Worse still, I could no longer afford to pay my bills. Things got pretty desperate very quickly after that.

Subconsciously I had given up. In fact, I was on the verge of quitting the company when Jim came to have a chat with me.

Jim said to me, 'How are you going to pay your mortgage this month?'

I told him that I had honestly no idea, although actually I knew for certain I couldn't pay my mortgage that month at all. Not even close.

Jim pressed me to find out how much my mortgage was. By this point, I, this once cocky salesperson, was squirming with embarrassment and admitted that the payment due was £200, which was a huge sum 36 years ago. Without missing a beat he said I'd probably need a bit of money on top of that and wrote me out a cheque for £400. I was gobsmacked, but will never forget that moment. It was a turning point for me. His faith in me made me stop and evaluate everything. I thought, hold on, John, if he thinks you are good enough to do this, you must find a way to hang on in there and survive. In my case that meant picking up the phone book night after night and making cold call after cold call for the next four weeks. It was desperately hard work and a hell of a lot of people said no. However, enough people said yes and I learned a very important lesson about survival.

There is always a way

There are many ways to make up the numbers and they will vary depending upon what you are selling. The most obvious way is to hit the phones as I did after Jim spurred me on, because it really does work. But, over the years, I have found many other avenues too.

For example, many years ago, I used to sell office equipment. I watched my existing clients like a hawk and if they had maintenance contracts I'd go and talk to them.

I'd say, 'I see you have this contract and just wanted to let you know that it is up for renewal in November and I would be more than happy to talk about it then.' I might also mention that the machine they had was a bit knackered and might need replacing at some point. Again, I always offered my help and advice.

My boss at the office equipment firm, Jim Higgins, used to say to me, 'Why are you wasting your time going to talk to people about these contracts that are not up for months? You should be doing other things.'

'Ah,' I said, 'you might be right, but at least I am constantly seeing people and talking to them.'

Sure enough, the moment the machine went kaput or the contract ended, the clients gave me a call and asked me in to see them. Within two years I became that company's top salesperson and within five years I was promoted to look after a huge district.

Mike, one of my then colleagues, said, 'Stone me, John's done it again! How come I am only getting in to see maybe eight people a week, whereas on average John gets to see 15 to 20?'

Jim said he thought it was because the thought had never occurred to John that people might not want to see him! In a way he was right. It has never occurred to me that people might not want to see me. That hasn't changed in 50 years. The real point is, even if some people don't want to see me, I know that if I lay the groundwork and make enough calls, there is someone else out there who will.

It doesn't matter what industry or business you are in; even when times are tough, there is always a way to get in to see people. Sometimes you may even have to be a bit cheeky. Early on in my career, I worked in the catering division of McVitie and Price, selling their biscuits to factories and warehouses around Nottingham. I was actually pretty good at it and was the firm's number one account opener, once opening 200 accounts in just eight weeks. However, there was one particular factory in Nottingham which I couldn't get anywhere near. The lady in charge of the canteen simply wouldn't take my call. I called and called. I wrote and wrote and tried every approach I could think of but couldn't get her to speak to me, let alone agree to an appointment. I became increasingly frustrated because it was a large factory employing 1,000 plus people and therefore had a big canteen. I knew that if I could get this contract, I would be on to a very good thing indeed.

One day I was standing outside the factory, wracking my brains as to what to do next, when I saw a delivery truck going in. Without a moment's hesitation, I ran round the blind side of the delivery truck while the driver was distracted talking to the fellow on the security gate. As the truck moved forward, I walked alongside it, keeping pace with the vehicle, which involved a bit of a jog as it picked up speed. Then, without anyone noticing, I darted into a side door of the factory. Panting a little, I walked up to one of the workers and asked politely if they could direct me to the canteen. Looking only a little surprised, they duly pointed me in the right direction. Just minutes later, bold as brass, I walked up to the woman I had been trying to see all along and introduced myself as John Cross from McVitie and Price.

She shrieked, 'How the hell did you get in?'

With a bit of a smile I told her that I was having no luck in trying to contact her, so I had seized my chance and slipped around the blind side of a delivery truck. To which she threw back her head and laughed.

'You cheeky little beggar,' she said, smiling. Then, to my joy, she added, 'Well, seeing as you are here you had better sit down and tell me what you have come here to say.'

I opened an account with that factory that very day and they went on to become one of McVitie and Price's best customers. That once elusive lady actually became quite friendly with me too and introduced me to quite a lot of other new customers. The point is: find a way in. There is always a way, and once you start thinking like this survival is assured.

Overcome fear and nervousness

Fear of the unknown is the one thing that holds most people back. Myself? I want to know everything about the unknown because the only thing we have to fear is fear itself, as Franklin D Roosevelt famously said during his inaugural address in 1933. I have always been able to come to terms with the unknown and conquer any fear. That, to me, is the key to survival.

The way I see it is, why would I worry about going out to make a sale today? What on earth is there to worry about? People might say 'no'. But they might just as easily say 'yes'. So why not knock on the door and find out? After all, if you don't knock on the door you will never find out either way. Never let fear hold you back. Learn to cope and deal with your fears and then they are no longer fears. It is that simple.

I believe that we all have the gift of a 'third eye', but most of us just don't use it. This third eye is in the brain and it is what helps us visualise things. If you learn to control this third eye, you can turn it around and look at things from a different perspective. You can use it to imagine what it is like from the outside looking in. Once you learn that, you can start to see things in a completely different way. That is how I have always overcome any fears. I take my third eye and think about where I will be in ten or 20 years' time. Then I imagine how I can get there and what I have to do. Then I do it. When you can do this, there is nothing in life that can knock you down. When there is nothing to weigh you down, there is nothing to be afraid of.

For a salesperson, one of the most debilitating character traits is being nervous about speaking to strangers. It is, after all, a skill that cuts straight to the heart of the job. I am lucky in that I have always been quite a confident person and love speaking in public.

When I was 11 years old, I used to speak regularly in school debates and I was often nominated to read from the Bible to the whole school in the mornings. Maybe inside I was nervous, but the important thing was that, to those on the outside, the words came out just fine. I also found that the more I did, the better I became, and once you get good at it you can feed off that adrenaline flow that comes from your audience.

If you feel that fear and nervousness of dealing with strangers is something that is holding you back, one of the most telling things to do is to video yourself talking in public. Trust me. You should try it. People who do this are often amazed when they look at the playback and see all the visual and verbal tics that hitherto they had no idea that they were doing. I once went on a training course for public speakers where the organisers did just this exercise. One of the guys that was there with me came out to the podium to speak and spent the entire 15 minutes holding his balls! He had no idea he was doing it. Subconsciously, he felt naked in front of the audience, so his body language was all about protecting himself. Do you think any one of us heard a word he was saying? Of course not; we were too busy suppressing embarrassed giggles.

If you are going to speak in public, whether it be one-to-one or to an audience of any size, you have to find a way to get over any innate embarrassment.

...but always do the right thing

I honestly believe that part of the reason I am successful is I only ever let people buy things that they should be buying from me and I don't let them buy things they shouldn't. I am always able to say to someone, hand on heart, that this product or that is absolutely right for them in their situation. I wholeheartedly believe that you have to be totally honest and have total integrity with all your clients. Any salesperson who does that will be ahead of the game.

When I talk to people, they always know it is the truth because it comes from the heart. When you are not afraid to speak from the heart, people will see you as something different from most other people. They will trust you.

One of the most important elements in survival is trust. If people don't trust you they will never, ever buy from you, no matter how good you think you are and how good your product appears to be. A golden rule for any salesperson is never to deviate from the truth or knowingly tell a lie. Being honest is so important. If you have not got that, people see through you straight away.

I will talk in more detail about honesty and trust later in this book, but it is important to say here that these qualities are a vital part of the survival process. If things are not going well and you are troubled by negative feelings, you should always take a good hard look at yourself to make sure you are doing the *right thing*. If, even for a moment, you think that you are not, then you should get out from under it straight away. You are not being fair to yourself, you are not being fair to your clients and you are not being fair to your company if you are selling a product that you do not believe is going to be right for everyone. If you cannot honestly say, I work for the best company, with the best products, to give my clients the best possible advantage, then you must change your job.

I always look upon doing the right thing as though it is a triangle. When I sell a product to a client, the client is always at the top of a triangle, the company I work for is at one corner of the base and I am at the other bottom corner. If I sell my clients the right product, the client will benefit, my company will benefit and John Cross will benefit. The moment I put myself there at the top, or my company at the top, and sell the poor client something

11

that is actually just going to get the figures up, that is when it all begins to unravel.

Potential clients will see it a mile off if you are insincere or don't really believe in what you are selling. However, if you do believe in what you are selling and love the company you work for, it is a pretty potent combination that cannot fail to impress.

I once went into a supermarket in the United States because Sherry and I had some precious gifts we wanted to bring back to the UK and needed some cardboard to pack them safely. For some reason, we couldn't find any cardboard or packaging anywhere, so I went into this supermarket and asked a guy who was stacking shelves: can you help? He was very pleasant and asked me to hold on a moment. Before very long, he returned with a couple of boxes. He asked me if the boxes he had found would do, and I said they'd do just great and thanked him profusely. Then, without being asked, he started to help me break them down. While we were doing that he said, 'What do you know about this store?'

I confessed that I did not know a lot and until that day had never even set foot inside his shop. This helpful chap then spent the next ten minutes telling me how good a store it was and what a marvellous company they were to work for. He came out with all sorts of facts, statistics and colourful historical detail. I was utterly spellbound. Here he was, a lowly employee of a large supermarket group, yet he was so immensely proud of the job that he had that he could not help but share it with a complete stranger. A complete stranger who was not even buying anything to boot. He utterly believed in what he did and the company he worked for, and that shone through for all to see. It was a truly humbling experience. If any salesperson could have only half of this man's enthusiasm about the products they sold and the company they worked for, their success would be virtually guaranteed.

You can't win them all

The final words on survival must surely be that you cannot win them all. Our ability to communicate with human beings is one of the most important qualities we have but, however good a communicator you are and however much you know or love your product, you won't be able to connect with everyone. Don't take it to heart. It is simply a fact of life. Accept it and move on.

Sometimes in my long sales career, although thankfully very rarely, I have met some people who are just not very nice or who are entirely negative about my products. Sometimes, inexplicably, the people I go to see seem very angry and resentful that I am there at all, even though they have requested to see me in the first place. When I meet people like that, I don't judge them. I comfort myself with the belief that their anger and hostility are usually masking some other problem and they are behaving like this to protect themselves. It is more likely than not that there is something behind the hardened exterior.

However, I don't immediately give up and stomp off in a huff. What is the point in that? Part of the survival process is to keep an open mind. My opening gambit in a situation like this is to say, 'Before we do anything, what has your previous experience been?'

It is quite likely that your disgruntled subject may say that they have previously been let down by a salesman and feel they were given bad advice. If you can put their mind at rest, then they will usually listen to you.

Occasionally, though, it is just not possible to penetrate their negative feelings. I have encountered this in the past. In such a situation, I pick up my briefcase, politely say that it seems we are not going to get on together and leave. If someone is going to become one of my clients, they have to be able to trust me and if they feel they can't, I'd rather they didn't deal with me. I never let it send me into a downward spiral, though. I always know that I have another appointment to go to. And, because I am well prepared, I always do.

Step Two: Consolidate

Many years ago I bought my wife Sherry a new car. Times were good, my sales career was taking off and it was, as it turned out, the second new car I had bought her in three years. I remember the day clearly. It was a bright, crisp Saturday in April and as Sherry drove us both back to our home in the brand new Ford Fiesta she was smiling broadly, clearly enjoying her new toy.

Then, suddenly, she turned to me and said, 'I wonder if there will be any flowers when I get home.'

I confess that for a few moments I was at a bit of a loss and racked my brains to see if I had somehow forgotten an important anniversary. At last, secure in the knowledge that I hadn't, I asked her why she was expecting a bouquet.

'Well, when we bought our other car from that same dealer three years ago, there was a beautiful bouquet waiting for us on our doorstep,' she said.

And there was, too. I had completely forgotten this, but Sherry never had. As a result, when the time came to upgrade her car, she didn't think twice about returning to the same dealer. In fact, for her, no other dealer would do. And, sure enough, when we got home that day, there were the flowers waiting for Sherry on the doorstep.

The clever folk at our local garage had realised that the simple device of delighting their female customers with a bunch of flowers would get them coming back time and again. They had, for very little outlay, secured a loyal customer, if not for life, at least for a very long time indeed.

In idle moments I have often thought about how I would become the world's greatest car salesperson. Witnessing Sherry's excitement at this bouquet made me realise that it would be ever so easy to sell a lot of motorcars to the same people over and over again. The first thing I would do would be to send them a birthday card on the anniversary of their buying the car. I would enclose a note in it that would say something like, 'Congratulations, you have had your car for one year and here is some information about our new range of family cars. Do come and see me any time if you want to have a test drive.'

After two years, I'd send a second card. 'Congratulations,' it would say. 'You have had the car for two years; here is some information about our new such and such model.'

I'd do it again on the third year, too. I am prepared to bet that if someone did that every year, on the anniversary of when their customer bought their car, the car buyer would be bowled over. Goodness, they will say, are those people at that car dealership different or what?

That little extra thought can make extra sales like you wouldn't believe, whatever discipline you are in. If I do business with a client who is referred, however small an investment they make, I always send a bottle of brandy as a thank you to the person who referred them. It costs me £70 for this bottle and I get their name printed onto the label. It is a special bottle and everyone loves it. Rest assured, when they have more money to invest or friends who need financial advice, they will think of me first.

This is all, for me, a perfect illustration of the second rule of succeeding in sales: you have to *consolidate*. Consolidation is all about building a base, putting all the things you do in the run up to a sale and beyond onto a firm footing. It is the foundation for everything to come.

The process of building a house gives us a perfect analogy for consolidation. When a builder starts putting up a house, the first thing he has to do is dig the foundations, lay in some concrete and then set down some blue bricks. For those not familiar with the house building trade: blue bricks are very hard, impervious structures with a high crushing strength and low water absorption. They are considered to be essential to the construction process because, without them, the whole house could come crashing down.

The consolidation process in sales is just like putting in those solid blue bricks and creating a base. It is about listening, setting goals, meeting targets and doing all the things that you said you were going to do.

Too many salespeople try to get from A to C without going through B, i.e. putting those basic building blocks in place. I can tell you now, it is very difficult, if not impossible, to sustain a successful sales career unless you put those blue blocks in.

Under-promise and over-deliver

In my experience of the sales industry, and as I have said I have been around for a while, everyone over-promises and under-delivers. They promise the Earth to their customers and then spectacularly fail to come up with the goods. I always make a point of doing exactly the opposite. I always under-promise and over-deliver. It is very easy to over-deliver. To over-deliver you just have to keep your word. You do what you say you would do. At the time and place that you said you would do it. It is that simple.

Under-promising and over-delivering is the easiest way to build a solid foundation with sales prospects. It is an action which will cost you nothing, just a little effort and organisation. Just do what you said you will do. It is such basic, simple stuff, but it makes all the difference in the world.

I will show you just how it works.

One year, I signed up half a million pounds' worth of business from a client who phoned the office over Christmas and said, 'I want to see John.' He had come to a seminar in Cambridge because he had a lot of money and wanted to do something with it. So off I went and in a short space of time the deal was done.

While I was there, I took the opportunity to ask why he was switching to me. The man explained that, up until now, he had been investing his money with a high street bank. Their original pitch for his investment had been marvellous, but after that, every time he had phoned to speak to his advisor, he had been put through to a different person. The person he had originally spoken to had moved on or been promoted and no one really 'owned' his case. Then, when the markets went down, he phoned to ask for a review of his investments. He wanted to have a discussion with someone, but the people on the other end of the line were ducking and diving and bobbing and weaving. Despite his persistence, he could never speak properly to anyone.

So he went elsewhere. I was lucky enough that he chose to come to one of my seminars and gave me a call. His experience with me was completely different. Every time he spoke to my office, I was there to speak to him. If I wasn't at my desk at the moment he called, I called him back by the end of the day. If he called between nine and five, he always got through to a real person, not a machine, and that person was always familiar with his case and keen to help. Plus, as I do with all my clients, I sent him quarterly valuations on his investments and kept him regularly updated on the state of the market.

He liked it. He liked that personal touch. He liked the fact I treated him with respect and understood his needs as a person and an individual. Everybody wants that. To me, that is the foundation of everything going forward. I always respond to a request. I always do what I say I will do and more if I can.

I always love it when I see examples of this elsewhere, because it is so rare. Mike Wilson, our company chairman, keeps a little notepad in his pocket; it is about 2 by 3 inches. Every single time someone says something to him that he needs to do something about, he gets the notepad out and writes it down. Then he does it. He is never ever without that notebook. Whatever method you use, everyone should be doing this. Always.

I always have a follow-through list of around 20 things that I have promised to do for clients. I can't always deal with them all in one day, because other things happen, but I always aim to get at least 15 items from my list dealt with and out of the way every single day. The next day I always start with the five I didn't deal with on the previous day and attend to them first. It is simple stuff, but amazingly not many people do it. They get too bogged down in other things.

Most salespeople do not follow through; they make promises and they don't keep them. They are rushing towards the next sale all the time instead of consolidating.

Listening to the verbal and non-verbal cues

Do you know one of the best things about consolidation? It is that your sales prospect actually does a lot of the hard work for you. All you need to do is pause your patter for a moment, pin back your ears and take some notice.

What I am talking about are verbal and non-verbal cues. We all give them off all the time. Think about it. If someone is saying something you like, you will sit forwards in your chair, look alert and perhaps even nod in agreement at certain key phrases. The way you use your hands while you speak is a great indicator of your true feelings too. If your hands are open in front of you, for example, it is generally a clear indication that you like what you are hearing.

At the other end of the scale, if you don't like what someone is saying, you will probably look and feel distracted. You may even fold your arms around yourself protectively, as if to shut the speaker out.

Experts have made an entire industry out of 'reading' people's body language, but you don't need to have gone on long courses or spent years at university to understand what someone is trying to tell you by their reactions. You just need to be receptive to it. In time, with experience, you will soon know what your prospect is trying to say through their body language and recognise the positive signals. A simple understanding of this will give you a whole lot to go on in building up those blue bricks towards a successful sale.

Verbal cues are a great base too. I don't mean when people say; 'Great, Mr Cross, where do I sign?' I mean when they tell you something that indicates that they want to do something, but have a few residual doubts. Sadly, too many salespeople confuse that something they say as an out-and-out 'no'.

Very often, in a sales situation, when people say 'no', what they actually mean is 'I am interested, but I need more information'. They haven't yet got enough information to make a decision. An inexperienced salesperson may think, harrumph, I have wasted my time; I'm off. However, a patient, experienced salesperson should recognise it as a clear cue that the blue bricks are almost in place, but there is more work to be done.

I am going to stick my neck out here, at the clear risk of falling foul of equal opportunities proponents, and say women are more

18

likely than men to say 'no' when actually what they really mean is they would like some further information while they weigh up their decision. I'll leave it to those behavioural experts to say why this might be, but my own theory is that after years of being let down by men they have become more cautious and wary. And perhaps rightly so.

Whatever the reason, I can say with some 50-years or more of experience on the road that, as a rule, women are far more analytical about what they buy and will generally prevaricate much longer than men. However, whether it is a woman or a man who is clearly cautious about buying my product, I will adjust my technique to take into account the clear verbal cues my would-be client has laid out for me.

I will break the sale down into its component parts and talk it through step-by-step in order to help them make that difficult decision. In my case, as a financial advisor, perhaps I will start by reminding them of their original aim to get capital growth from their savings and the fact that they have already agreed that they are unlikely to get that from a bank or building society these days. I might lighten the mood by thanking them very much for the £300,000 they have been so diligently keeping in the building society. Coincidently, my daughter Heidi borrowed £300,000 from that very same building society to buy her family home, I might say. I will add that Heidi has already made a £200,000 profit on the deal thanks to someone else's money, thank you very much!

The next step is to take the cautious would-be customer even further down the road. Reminding them again of their desire for capital growth, I will ask if it is investing the whole £300,000 that is making them nervous. Would it be better to start off with, say, an investment of £150,000? By this stage, they might start nodding. Fine, I'll say, we'll come back to the other £150,000 later on. More nodding. On the other hand, I might continue, as you are talking about £150,000 and I am talking about £300,000, why don't we meet down the middle at £225,000? You'd be amazed by how many people, after you have broken the sale down into its component parts and gently led them through it, say, 'OK, let's do that then.' It is all about cutting the cloth according to the person you are with. But, while I have walked away with an investment of £225,000, how many salespeople would have left when their client first started wavering? Quite a few, I'll wager.

It doesn't matter if you are selling financial products or cars; the principles are always the same. Always listen to your clients, because they will be trying to help you do your job.

Learning to speak to people

Learning how to speak to people is just as important in laying those foundations as knowing how to listen. Oh, come on, John, you might be saying, I have been speaking since I was 12 months old and I am pretty good at it now. But I wonder if you really are?

I confess that I don't think I really learned to speak to people properly until my very first job when I joined a wholesale grocer in Leicester in 1963. Working at Roberts and Roberts as a young lad with no experience of sales was the greatest thing that ever happened to me. The boss, Ray Ogilvy, sat me down in an office with a telephone and said to me, 'Right, John, get on that phone and speak to people.' I hadn't really used a phone much before, so I was a little daunted, but I am never afraid of giving something a go. So it became my job on Monday mornings to phone 50 people from first thing at 8.45am. I still remember my initial patter today.

'Good morning, Mr Smith, it is John Cross from Roberts and Roberts,' I would say. 'Have you got any orders today?'

If they said no, I would thank them, wish them good day and move on to the next call.

'Good morning, Mr Brown, it is John Cross from Roberts and Roberts. Have you got any orders today? No? Well, thank you very much; I will call next week.'

'Good morning, Mr Clarke, it is John Cross from Roberts and Roberts. Have you got any orders today?'

Then, gradually, I learned how to speak to people better. I learned how to strike up a rapport and gain their trust. Once I did that, no one minded that I mentioned special offers, or that they might like to try something else. In fact, they were grateful for my thoughtfulness.

'Oh,' they would say. 'Thank you, John, for telling me about that. That sounds like a great idea.'

20

Because I got good at talking to people and clearly enjoyed talking to strangers as well as established clients, I very quickly developed a reputation as the person to talk to in the order office. Very soon, every person that called in would ask for me by name, regardless of which other poor salesperson picked up the call.

'Where is John?' they would say. 'Is John there? I want to speak to John.'

I am sure it must have been very frustrating for my erstwhile colleagues, but I was speaking to these people in a way that they liked, so it made sense that they asked for me. Of course, what happened next was that these happy customers were eager to feed back to Ray that I was a bright, personable guy who was clearly very switched on. So, at the tender age of 19, I was put out on the road. Roberts and Roberts never used to put anyone out until their mid-twenties, but they could see that I had something different about me and were quite rightly quick to exploit it. This was now my opportunity to learn how to transfer all the skills I had learned over the phone into speaking to people face-to-face. As always, I grasped the opportunity with both hands and quickly built an even better rapport with the people I came into contact with.

I never got bored of speaking to new people. I could see dozens of people every day and still be fascinated by what every one of them had to say, whether they were talking about the weather, the political situation or last night's footie results. In among the small talk, I learned how to ask the right probing questions to find out what they liked or didn't like. I learned very early on that a salesperson does not 'talk' people into buying. There is no point in trying to manipulate people. If you want them to be happy, and more importantly to keep on buying from you, you need to understand their real emotional needs. You will find all that out if you talk to them like real people, and then you can really start to lay the foundations for a real, solid, long-term relationship.

Keeping your foundations solid and straight

I'd like to end this chapter with a strong note of caution. Denigrating the competition is not a blue brick. Never seek to lay the foundation of your future relationship with a client by attacking their previous choices. Aside from being completely unprofessional and a clear sign of weakness, it is highly likely to completely backfire on you.

If a client says to me they have been dealing with one of my competitors for the last 15 years, I always say that I am delighted to hear it. If I instantly retorted, 'What, that bunch of shysters? What were you thinking of dealing with them? No wonder you are not happy,' I would effectively be telling my client to his or her face that they have been a complete idiot for a decade and a half.

Never, ever, demean a client by suggesting they are stupid to buy from your competitors. It would be utterly self-defeating.

I always turn the conversation around and subtly find out if they have had any problems with their former company. After acknowledging my competitor and giving them credit for what they are, I might say something like, 'Tell me, have you got the same chap dealing with you that you started with?' If they say, oh no, there have been a few changes, all of a sudden the truth will emerge. Instead of going in with all guns blazing and telling them they are a fool, with a little probing, I have found the Achilles' heel of my competitor and can now go on to happily lay my own foundations by correcting all the things that I now know niggle my prospect about their former choice of supplier.

It is upon these strong foundations that a successful sale is built and maintained.

Step Three: Move forward

Over 30 years ago I worked alongside a colleague called Stevie Marsh who was an utterly brilliant and gifted salesman. Unfortunately, he was utterly useless in every other department and totally disorganised, but that is a different story.

The reason I remember Stevie so clearly and with such fondness is that he gave me a gift which has been the foundation for all my subsequent successes in sales. He showed me how to move my sales forward to the next level.

I had spotted early on that Stevie was a successful salesperson with tons of natural ability and watched him closely to find out what his secret might be. I quickly discovered that he was holding sales seminars for potential prospects and asked him if I might come along to one to observe. Stevie was a lovely, generous chap and readily agreed.

I remember the evening of Stevie's seminar in London's busy Kingsway as clearly as though it were yesterday. The seminar was being held in one of those large, anonymous hotels, common to the area, on a bitterly cold February evening. I thought I had better make myself useful, so, as people came through the door, I played doorman and took their winter coats and hung them on the rail. I couldn't believe what I was seeing. In a matter of moments, I had hung up 70 coats. I was utterly gobsmacked. Those 70 coats added up to 70 complete strangers who had made the journey through an inhospitable winter's evening just to hear my colleague Stevie talk. It was amazing. All he had done was put an advert in the London Evening Standard and he had got this brilliant turnout of eager prospects. I could hardly wait to see what he would do next.

Now, Stevie, bless him, was so disorganised that he didn't know what he was going to do or say next himself. He didn't seem to have planned this far. He stood there in front of the group of 70 and said, 'What shall we talk about? Money?' And that was exactly what he did. Luckily, he was so charismatic and such a gifted salesperson that the whole thing flowed from there and the evening was an enormous success. I was utterly hooked. I knew I was not only in the presence of greatness, but also being shown the path to almost guaranteed success in sales.

I immediately asked Stevie if he would mind if I began seminars of my own and he said he had no problem with it whatsoever. Indeed, Stevie led such a chaotic existence that he stopped doing the seminars himself very soon afterwards, even though they had been a runaway success. For me, though, this was the start of something very big which has sustained my career ever since.

If you are still not convinced, do the maths. If I can get 70 people (and sometimes more) to turn up to one of my seminars, that is 70 people listening to my story. If I only did that once a month, that would be just shy of 1,000 new prospects every year ready to hang on to my every word. The odds are also high that I can convert a great deal of this very willing audience into being my clients because, don't forget, they are voluntarily attending a seminar, so they are clearly keen to buy. What salesperson wouldn't want that?

To return to the analogy which opened this book, my seminars are keeping my hopper permanently filled with prospects and are regularly topping it up. That is how you move your sales process into top gear.

Salespeople should always be in motion and looking forward to see how they can improve their lot. If you are on the move, you tend to be creating something. If you are in motion, you will be out there and trying new things all the time. You should never sit back and never be complacent. You should always be out there trying to find a new way, or new client.

There is always a way to move forward, even in the tough times. Although the seminars have been an enormous success for me over the years, I have never stopped looking for new, innovative ways to keep my hopper full to overflowing.

When we hit the big financial crisis in 2008, many salespeople struggled and it seemed even worse because we had all had such a great year the year before. At one stage, I was 40% down. I didn't crumble, though. I sat down and thought about how to deal with it and how to move forward.

The answer I came up with was to be *useful* to my clients, which was an idea given to me by my strategic coach Dan Sullivan. I kept in touch and offered all the help, advice and reassurance they needed. I figured that if someone took the trouble to be useful to them during this terrible period, at the end of it they would remember who helped them and reassured them. I was the one who was there when they needed someone. Sure enough, when we emerged from that dark period, they remembered me. Many of my other sales colleagues kept their heads low, just in case their clients called and withdrew all their cash. It has therefore taken them much longer to recover.

There is little point in ducking behind the parapet hoping things will 'just get better' or your sales margin will marginally improve. They won't unless you do something about it yourself and do something to keep things moving. If you want to unparalyse yourself, be in motion, be interested and be useful.

Visualise

My dad said to me when I was a young boy, 'Son, if you have to sweep the streets, be the best street sweeper that there has ever been.'

That pronouncement has stayed with me all my life and has influenced everything I have ever done. I have always tried to be the best at whatever I have turned my hand to and every job I have undertaken. I can't imagine why anyone would not want to give their best. Why would anyone go home every day knowing that they had undersold themselves? Why would they not make that extra bit of effort in order to make that extra bit of difference? This is what it is all about. You can't move forward in sales if you don't do everything that is in your power to be the best every single day, day in and day out.

Many people don't believe that it is that simple. It is. If you have got a view of where you are and where you want to be, then concentrate on that. Don't get diverted. Not by anything. Many salespeople suffer from getting diverted too easily. They are a bit like butterflies; they flutter here and flutter there and get around.

25

There is nothing wrong with being a flutterer, because you get to see a lot of people and may even get lots of business. But fluttering on its own is not enough to become the best.

Salespeople who suffer from this syndrome go through a process something like this: they have a new product and it is exciting. They metaphorically put some ribbon around it and go straight out to see people and sell some of this fabulous product with hardly a backwards glance. Then, after a while, they get to thinking that this once amazing product is now stale and old hat. They go off to look for another more exciting product. Then, after a while, they get bored of that one and flutter on to another. And so on and so on.

The thing that our flutterers seem to forget about being a salesperson is: if you get excited about an idea, invariably the person you are dealing with will get excited about the same idea. Excitement is infectious. Unfortunately, salespeople don't retain their enthusiasm.

If you want to be successful there is no point in being a flash Harry. You need to be consistent. You need to do what you do over and over, week by week and year by year. I am always excited about my products, just as I am excited about life, and I am in for the long haul on both!

One of my favourite quotes is: 'I know where my place is in the universe and I am comfortable there.' I am genuinely happy with the time and space I occupy. There are very few people who ever seem to think about the time and space they occupy in the universe, because they are too busy going pell-mell onto the next thing.

You have to be able to do more than just flutter. You need direction, purpose and tenacity. That is what puts you ahead of the crowd.

To get out of the 'fluttering cycle', it really helps to visualise the place where you want to be. It works. Every time.

I have, myself, always used visualisation technique to great effect. I'll give you an example. When my company announced some 30 years ago that they would be holding a conference in America for their highest grossing salespeople, I knew that I had to be there when it took place late the following year. So what did I do? I made it the focal point of everything that I did. It was my first thought every morning and my last thought at night before I went to sleep. Central to this vision was a picture of the very hotel where the conference was to be held, which I cut out from a brochure. The hotel itself was a very grand affair, set in front of a golden sand beach with azure blue waves lapping at its edge and surrounded by lush palm trees. I could almost feel the wind in my hair and feel the warmth of the Californian sun on my face every time I looked at this photo.

To push me on still further, I stuck this picture onto my sales graph on my office wall. I placed it at the very point that coincided with the number of sales I would have to get in order to realise my dream. That way, whenever I checked my graph, or merely glanced at the wall behind me, there it was, a gleaming beacon inviting me to work harder. It was a daily, even hourly, reminder of my ultimate goal.

Sure enough, I managed to reach that goal and that year found myself in that very hotel, living my dream and dipping my toes in that azure blue water. Inspired, I used this method for all my other goals, large and small. Pretty soon, my sales graph became littered with pictures. One photo was of a shining, hand-built Jensen Interceptor sports car. I thought it was a fantastic car. It was the only time I had really been interested in cars, so on the board it went. Another was a rather jolly picture of a smiling Mickey Mouse. Sherry and I had long wanted to treat the kids to a trip to Disneyland in America, so the famous cartoon mouse found a home half way up my sales graph.

This may all sound rather comical, even childish, but it acts as a constant and inspiring reminder. If you want not just to sell, but to sell well and be the best, then you need to visualise what your rewards will be, so that you can really put your mind to it. That is the way to keep moving forward.

One sale always leads to another

Seminars are not the only way to keep the sales hopper full and you on your way to realising those well-visualised dreams, either. I have always found that, with a bit of hard work and ingenuity, one sale will always lead to another. After all, if you have one happy customer, it makes perfect sense for them to do some of the work for you and help you find another. It has always worked brilliantly for me.

I'll give you another great example. Early on in my sales career, when I was selling office equipment such as automated calculating machines, I got in with a group of shoe manufacturers in Northampton. They seemed very happy with the product, so I asked the executive I dealt with whether he had any thoughts on who else in the shoe industry I should be talking to. I was acutely aware that in this industry, as in any other, even fierce rivals often knew each other quite well, and often got on well too when they weren't vying for important orders. Sure enough, my client very helpfully provided me with a list of people I might like to approach.

The very next day, I was on the phone.

'Hello, Mr Smith, Mr Brown from Acme Shoes Inc. has just bought one of our latest automated calculating machines and mentioned to me that it might be of interest to you,' I said.

Invariably, the Mr Smiths of this world were so incensed that their rivals had a better, more new-fangled gizmo than they did that they would order one almost immediately so as not to be left behind. It works. It really does. You just have to make the call.

I didn't stop at the list of recommendations provided by my first client, either. After exhausting his list, I went to the library and got a directory of all the other shoe and boot manufacturers in the area. I then painstakingly telephoned them all, one by one, and told them about my product. I also added the fact that Mr Smith and Mr Brown now both had one and asked if they thought they might like to take a look too. I vividly remember one company secretary almost exploding with rage at the thought that Mr Smith, a smaller competitor, was stealing a march on him with some new piece of technology. He ordered ten automated calculating machines on the spot!

I have used adaptations of this technique with all the industries I have ever been in and it has never failed to work.

A further little trick I'd like to share with you comes from another golden rule of mine. When I am going to see a regular client, I never, ever take the same route twice. I learned this when I was on the road for McVitie and Price, travelling around and meeting people at various office canteens to sell my wares. I found that if I took a different route, I would often come across a road filled with offices or factories that I had not seen before. It stood to reason that many of these offices or factories had canteens too, or at least some sort of catering facility for the hundreds of staff who clearly worked there. All I had to do was take a note of the address and give them a call.

One day, when I was selling automated calculating machines, I got completely lost while trying out a new route and found the biggest factory I had ever seen. Prior to that day, I had had no idea that the street existed, let alone this factory. I was so excited that I stopped my car and walked straight into reception to introduce myself. The receptionist seemed a little taken aback and said the company secretary would only ever see people by appointment.

'Fine,' I said, with a broad smile. 'Would you mind giving me his details?'

She did and within a week I was in front of him, showing him my products. I got a really good sale out of that visit and still remember the glow of pride I felt when I walked out of that factory. I thought to myself, how many people who worked on this patch before me had never even bothered to drive down this road? I did, even if it was by accident, and look what happened to me.

I used the same technique when I started selling financial products. While I was driving to appointments, I took a note of all the addresses with 'For Sale' boards outside. The next day I would be on the phone, saying I could see they were in the process of moving and did they need any help with finding a mortgage or dealing with the financial arrangements? By striking while the iron was hot, so to speak, I got a fair few contracts.

Just keeping your eyes open can make one contract blossom into many more, with the minimum of effort.

PPP: Proper prior preparation

I'm always gobsmacked by the number of salespeople who are prepared to fly by the seat of their pants. Perhaps they are so relieved to get in front of a client that they forget the important bit is to actually prepare for the event. They don't seem to realise that if they don't know what they are talking about it will stand out a mile. Apart from anything else, if you don't take the time to prepare, it makes that hard-won meeting a bit of a waste of time.

When I go to see a client it is proper prior preparation, or PPP, all the way. Nothing else will do.

As I will explain in more detail in the next section of this chapter, I always get all of my potential clients to fill out their fact-finding forms before our first meeting, which gives me full details of their current financial situation. Then I study it. Really study it. To me, it is not just a fancy form to keep regulators happy. It is full of vital clues to their attitude to finance, their appetite for risk and their hopes and aspirations for the future. I can see their full cash position set out before me, from what their property is worth to the spread of their investments and even what they are planning to do with their assets when they die. This is an incredibly valuable document and anyone would be a fool not to use it for some real, in-depth PPP.

PPP works for whatever product you are selling. At McVitie and Price, my PPP was a box of biscuit samples. I'd walk into shops, offices and factories with a case of digestives and ask the person in charge to try one. Most of the time I'd offer one to the other customers or staff too. Sometimes I'd get an order and sometimes I wouldn't, but my PPP was, in this case, getting me and my product out there. That is all you have to do.

Assume the close

Sound, long-term business relationships begin when both parties are fully committed. Every sales call should end with a specific agreement or commitment to take action, otherwise it is a waste of everyone's time. I am not visiting potential clients to make a new friend, although I have gone on to make many good long-term friends in my career. No, the reason I see a client is to make a sale. I always assume that the reason I am there to meet a client is to close the business, or why else would I be there? The secret to this is to make sure that all meetings have a definite purpose. I never, ever fly kites on the off chance that I may win the business.

It is for this very reason that I always take great pains to qualify my sale before the first meeting. To do this, I set out to find out as much information as possible, as early as possible. People say to me, oh, John, why do you do that? Surely you will put the client off by asking all sorts of personal details before you have gone in there to work your magic? This perplexes me. Surely the only way a sales relationship works is if you are both in it together? Aside from the fact that the financial regulations are such that it is a prerequisite to have such information on file, it makes sense to me to get all of this out in the open at the earliest possible opportunity.

Experience tells me that if you ask people for information in the right way and in a pleasant manner, they will usually give it to you. So I ask my would-be clients to fill in a very detailed fact-finding questionnaire before our first face-to-face meeting, in order to give me some idea of their current position. If they appear a little nervous about revealing such personal details, I lighten the mood by calling it a financial X-ray and that often helps. I tell them that I need to take a 'financial X-ray' because I cannot move them forward and help them achieve their goals and objectives if I don't know their current position.

Most people can see the sense in this, especially if they have already taken up their own time in order to visit one of my seminars. Most of the time I will have their full information even before our first meeting or, at the very least, I will walk in the door to a pleasant greeting accompanied by the words, 'Here are your forms, Mr Cross.'

This means that I can see straight away what their position is and what I should be talking to them about. It also means that this initial meeting is almost a closing interview where the client will inevitably go to signing the application forms.

You may say, that sounds too easy. It is almost an assumed close. You'd be right. All my meetings are always an assumed close – and it is as easy as preparing well in advance.

I make sure I only ever see people with certain attributes and, most importantly, a certain amount of money. I am able to choose who I see. You might say, John, you couldn't have always been like this. But I have. If you qualify your clients, you will only ever see the ones that meet your criteria. You will then do more business because, by definition, you will have got rid of all the chaff and will only be left with the wheat.

Listen and be patient

There is an old adage which goes something like: he who speaks first loses. I think that sums up many of the eager young turks I see, who think they are fabulous salespeople, yet who somehow don't seem to sell very much all the same. They are so busy jabbering away with their carefully honed patter that they don't pause to let the poor client draw breath, let alone say what their hopes, needs and aspirations may be. These oh-so-chatty salespeople jump in too quickly and talk and talk and talk, perhaps in a bid to be in control of the meeting. Yes, you need to be in control, but there are subtler ways to do this: ones that don't involve battering your client over the head with an endless stream of chatter in your enthusiasm.

When I go to a first meeting with a client, I am usually pretty secure in the knowledge that, if they have been to one of my seminars, they have already heard all about the products I sell and why they meet some of their goals. So, as I have taken care of that side of things and I have their precious fact-finding form, I let them do the talking. I will keep my opening remarks as brief as thanking them for coming to the seminar. Then it is over to them with a simple question like asking what it was that they heard at the seminar that interested them. It is not that I have nothing to say or haven't got bags of ideas; it is just that I want to hear what they have to say first.

This technique doesn't just go for the opening of a meeting, either. I am always careful to leave my prospects with enough time to give their honest reaction, even to the extent that I am content to sit in complete silence for several minutes while they gather their thoughts.

The art of being a great salesman and moving things on is centred in being a great listener. It is my firm belief that it is demeaning to a client to push them too hard. It is, after all, ultimately their decision. If the shoe were on the other foot, you'd hate to be badgered that hard, wouldn't you?

This is not for one moment to say that I don't push them towards the desired end point. Of course I do. I am there to do a job, after all. However, I do it in a subtle way. I liken my approach to building a small fire beneath my prospect and then providing enough fuel to allow the flames to gently flicker away.

If a client seems to be blowing this way and that, I will help them by gradually recapping what they have previously said. I will say something like, 'You told me that your number one priority was to reduce your inheritance tax. Can I just check something? Has that desire changed at all?'

I might go on to ask whether it is likely that their inheritance liabilities, which currently stand at, say, £250,000, will remain the same or increase.

At this point, I will stop and say nothing at all and let them respond. If I am still getting nowhere, I may finish the meeting by saying that I really don't mind if they decide to do nothing, but please, please do not make a decision by default. I have known far too many people who make a decision by default. They mean to get around to it, but they never do and so they are actually making a decision to do nothing by default. This will probably strike a real chord with the prospect, because we are all guilty of making decisions by default and usually bitterly regret our lack of action.

I only ask them to do one thing, and that is come back to me in the next week or ten days. They can say yes or no. I won't be offended. I just want them to let me know. I then ask my office to call them in ten days' time to ask them if they want to take it further or leave it for now.

Then I leave it in their court. I have listened, explained their options and gently fanned the flames. Now it is entirely up to them. I just leave the bonfire burning and they can come back to me. They can put the flames out straight away, or come back after ten days because it has been nagging away at them. They also know I won't chase them or harass them during any of this time. It is that simple.

This is a call to action, but it is not bludgeoning them over the head with a blunt instrument or talking into submission. If you want to get a prospective client to do something, you have to give them a reason, not simply shout in their ear until they give in. The way you do this is by establishing needs, goals, ambitions and targets. And I don't mean your goals; I mean theirs.

The way to move people forward is to help them to see the logic of what is being proposed to them.

Step Four: Self-education

My uncle Derek was an engineer who worked for a company called Jones and Shipman, which supplied machines that made other machines. His job was to visit various different factories to talk to the owners when the machines went wrong, or when they needed a new one. I went to stay with him for a while, as a very young man, and he asked me if I would like to accompany him to work. I thought this sounded like a great idea and spent all day with him, going from factory to factory, watching what he did and how he did it among the bustle and noise. I can still remember the heady smell of Swarfega, grease and oil even now.

At the end of the busy day, Derek turned to me and said, 'I am sorry, John, you were probably bored out of your brain.'

I wasn't, though. I was thrilled to bits. I had had a great day because I had learned so much. I learned something new almost every minute and to me learning something new is the most important thing there is in life.

This is a philosophy I have carried with me all my life and which has served me very well indeed in my working career. Although I wanted to be a salesman for as long as I can remember, I was not born a salesman. I have had to work hard for everything I have achieved. As I said at the beginning of this book, I spent my childhood years in a council house in Leicester and had no real advantages, except for being able to think and speak fast on my feet, which was quite useful in school debates.

However, even if someone does start with very little, you can train them to be successful. We all start with certain strengths and certain weaknesses. It is simply a question of finding or recognising those strengths and working hard to build them up and make them work effectively for you.

When I got my first job in selling soon after I left school, at Roberts and Roberts, wholesalers to the grocery trade, I realised that I had to educate myself above the norm if I wanted to be a success. I applied to the Grocers' Institute to see if there were any exams that I could take that would enable me to learn more about my new occupation. I already knew a fair bit about it because I had helped out in a shop from 11 years of age to earn a few pennies, but I was eager to know more.

I found out that there was a course, which would be followed by a short exam, and immediately signed up for it. The most memorable part of the course was when the Grocers' Institute used to send me all sorts of food samples from tea to sultanas for me to try. Over time I gradually learned how to distinguish between all sorts of flavours, textures and smells. Eventually, after much tasting, smelling and studying, I took the exam and became an associate of the Grocers' Institute. I was very proud to put this on my business card, which now said 'John Cross AGI'.

This immediately got me noticed. All around Roberts and Roberts I could hear people saying, well, this chap John Cross is only young, but look how ambitious he is. He's gone out there and off his own bat he is already an associate of the Grocers' Institute. An associate!

I think that course had a fair bit to do with the fact that I got promoted very quickly. The chaps at Roberts and Roberts recognised that I was a dynamic person who was prepared to go out and go the extra mile. It certainly distinguished me from my less enthusiastic colleagues.

My quest for knowledge did not end there. I then decided that I wanted to learn even more about the art of marketing and selling, so I cast my net to see what other courses I could do to help me in my quest. I found out that it was possible to do an extensive course which, at the end, would entitle me to become a member of the Institute of Marketing. To do this, I had to attend night school twice a week for seven years, with an exam at the end of every academic year. It was hard work, particularly while I was working long hours at my day job, but what spurred me on was the fact that it gave me a lot of valuable knowledge I didn't already have. At the end of those seven years, when I had successfully passed all of the exams, I proudly added MInstM to my business card, alongside the AGI.

Aside from helping me understand what I was doing, my qualifications really helped me stand out from the crowd. They also helped with my next career move, when I decided to come out of the grocery business and applied to join an office equipment firm. At the interview the people at the office equipment firm commented that I seemed to be really switched on and know what I was doing. They really appreciated the fact that I had made the effort to educate and improve myself and could see that I would be a real asset.

Shortly after I landed the office equipment job, the firm brought out a range of electronic calculating machines. It might sound old-fashioned now, particularly to a generation brought up on computers and smartphones, but these were the days before gadgets were commonplace and these electronic calculating machines were state of the art for their time. I really wanted to be on top of my game and understand what I was dealing with, so I went into the office early on a Saturday morning. No one else was around and I sat there from eight o'clock in the morning until late in the afternoon, learning everything I could about these new calculators. I did not go home until I understood completely what they could do, how they did it and where they might come in handy for any of my potential clients. My persistence paid off and in no time at all I became that firm's top salesperson, selling dozens and dozens of these calculating machines.

Not long after that, the same firm brought out a machine called the Statistician. This time, I didn't even have to go in to the office over the weekend, because one of the papers from my past Institute of Marketing course had been all about statistics and I had spent a year studying them in excruciating detail. I instantly felt completely at home with all the statistical formulas that were clearly baffling my colleagues and went out and sold the Statistician by the barrow-load. Once again, I was the top salesperson.

A few years later, as my career took off, I switched firms again and began what was to be a long stint in the financial services industry. The very first thing I did was look up all the courses available on shares and investing, and I ended up enrolling on a three-year course at the local technical college.

There I learned about loan stock, ordinary stock, preferences, gilts and anything and everything to do with the markets.

Guess what? Almost a month after I had passed my final exams, my company brought out something called the Share Exchange Scheme. Many of my fellow salespeople in the company did not have a clue how it worked and could barely hide the fact that they were very uncomfortable about the whole thing. But for me it was resoundingly simple because, thanks to my course, I understood all the ins and outs of complex financial transactions. I could see clients and confidently explain the Share Exchange Scheme because I knew exactly what I was talking about. I had no fears that I was going beyond my comfort zone, as so many of my colleagues did. I could tell my clients that if they give me these shares of theirs, I could give them a better return. You will not be surprised to learn that I did loads and loads of business on the back of that. Meanwhile, many of my less informed colleagues didn't even bother to mention the scheme to their clients, for fear of tying themselves up in knots.

Of course, when I signed up for my course in shares and investing, I had no idea that my company would be bringing out a complex Share Exchange Scheme. Just as I had no idea when I did my Marketing Institute course that it would give me essential knowledge about statistics, which would make me such a successful office equipment salesperson. The point is that both courses, indeed all the courses I have ever been on, have done something amazing for my career.

My colleagues have often said, 'Aren't you lucky you did a course on statistics/share exchange just right when you needed it?' But it was nothing to do with luck. It was all about hard work, a thirst for knowledge and a desire to constantly educate myself. It was not always easy, particularly with the demands of a young family too, but I always made the time to learn more and still do even to this day.

I have done this because I have always been a passionate believer in learning as much as I can about whatever it is that I am doing. I have never been content just to go with the flow. Perhaps I am just naturally inquisitive. Even going back to my childhood when my dad was making sausages, I wanted to know all there was to know about making sausages. What are the ingredients? How do you make them? What is the difference between this type and that? I have never stopped asking those sorts of questions ever since.

Continuously self-educating can have a massive, massive, impact on your life, especially as a salesperson. If you know your stuff and a client asks you a question, it gives them a huge amount of confidence in you if you can immediately reply with authority. If you don't answer the question because you can't, it simply exposes you as weak and foolish.

It doesn't matter what you are selling, either. If I had been a car salesman, I know I would have been the number one salesperson in the UK, because I understand what it is you need to do to become the number one car salesman in the UK. I know nothing about cars right now, but that is not relevant. I know about the people who buy cars and I would darn well do my utmost to go out and find out all the rest that I didn't know.

I always ask people, why would you not want to educate yourself? Why would you not want to know as much as you could about as wide a range of subjects as possible? Apart from anything else, I am quite sure that if I had not learned so much, I would never have enjoyed my jobs half so much.

Success in sales is all down to the way you are, how you treat your clients and how much you know. The principles hold true right across the board. If you want to be the best, you just have to be prepared to get out there and learn as much as you can. Self-education never stops; there is always something new to learn.

Recognise your strengths

I have for many years visited Dan Sullivan, an inspiring strategic coach who is based in Toronto in Canada and Chicago in the United States. I don't have to. Do you think I need a sense of purpose? Do you think I need to be told what I need to do to go forward? No, I don't. I don't need any of that stuff. I am already educating myself in other ways of going forward, understanding new things and exposing myself to ideas I have not been exposed to before.

The reason I work with Dan is simply another aspect of my constant search to improve myself. Dan has opened my mind to many new theories and ways of looking at the world, and that to me is important. I am always ready to learn more.

One of Dan's theories which has struck the greatest chord with me is this: what holds most people back is that our entire education system is geared towards showing us that we have strengths and weaknesses and that what really needs to be done to improve our lot is correcting the weaknesses. Guess what? After several miserable years at school, most people grow up to discover that their weaknesses are still weaknesses. What we should be doing is spotting our strengths, building them up and delegating our weaknesses to someone who can deal with them more effectively.

Short of effecting a 180-degree turn in our schools system, which is probably not in most people's gift and is certainly not in mine, the only solution to this daft obsession with tackling weaknesses is for us to take charge of our own destinies. We all need to find our strengths and work on them. I certainly have lived my life by this maxim, and if you do this you'll be amazed what you can achieve.

Playing to your strengths and delegating your weaknesses can help with so many aspects of your daily life. For example, a colleague who was a moderately successful salesperson bemoaned to me the fact that I had a chauffeur who has looked after me for the last 15 years and he wished he had a chauffeur too. He believed that if he had a chauffeur, he could use his time more effectively, working in the car going to and from meetings and clocking up more sales appointments.

'Well, get one,' I said, slightly perplexed as to why we were having this conversation because he could certainly afford it.

'No,' he said ruefully. 'I just can't.'

After a brief discussion, I got to the bottom of the problem. It turned out that he got car sick if he was not driving and particularly when he sat in the back of cars. I asked him if he would do something for me and he agreed.

I said, 'Sit in the back of a car for a month and *train* yourself to be able to work and not feel queasy.'

This chap wasn't terribly enthusiastic, but he agreed to give it a try for a month. After three weeks he emailed me to let me know how it was going. He said that in the first week he had felt terrible and had, in fact, been really sick. By the second week he had managed to spur himself on enough to feel a bit better and by the third week he was fine. He had managed to train himself and, as a result, was being happily driven around the country while he worked away in the back of the car. He was now working far more productively and converting his sales prospects with a new vigour as his soaring sales commission record bore witness.

It is amazing what you can do if you recognise your strengths. If all salespeople concentrated on their strengths they would find that, very easily, they would soon get all the answers to their questions about how to succeed in sales.

Never stop learning

Every year, for the last 36 years, I have been to Million Dollar Round Table (MDRT) in America. The MDRT is a sales club for the top salespeople in the world and only 5% of all the people who work in financial services are good enough to qualify for the MDRT. I have been very fortunate in that I also qualify for the top table, so I am in the top 1% of that 5% who go there.

I go to the annual MDRT event for a week to hear people who are bigger and better than me talk. I want to listen to their experiences. I want to hear their stories. I want to find out how they survived against seemingly insurmountable odds and what inspired them to do that. Anyone who is fortunate enough to go there will hear some amazing stories if they are prepared to pin their ears back and listen. Thanks to the MDRT, I've seen some of the greatest speakers in the world and have been continuously motivated and inspired by the things that I have heard.

Yet I have spoken to others who have been invited who are utterly cynical about this.

'Who wants to go all the way to America for all that bullshit?' they'll say. That amazes me. In my view, they are missing out on something that could improve them and make them stand head and shoulders above all their peers. Who wouldn't want that?

Anybody you meet can teach you something if you are but prepared to listen. Indeed, I strongly believe that you can learn something from anyone and everyone. Not all of my ideas are my own ideas. Many are ideas that I have stolen from other people. I am not embarrassed about it. I take other people's ideas, but I take them more seriously than anyone else and make them work for me. Good salesmen are not very often original, but they can pick up on other people's ideas and use them. There is no shame in that.

I was lucky enough to be born with some natural ability and enthusiasm, but I also had the desire to train and educate myself. I also realise that, however good I get, I can always get better.

I always learn from every experience and try to do a bit better the next time. In the early days of running my sales seminars, I made loads of mistakes. Looking back, I now see that some of them were quite ridiculous, but I learned my lessons step-by-step.

One of my very first events was held in a lovely hotel in Bury St Edmunds which overlooked a quaint market square. When I first went to look it over, everything looked great. By way of belt and braces, I made sure we checked that there were adequate car parking facilities for all of our guests. I found that, what with the hotel car park and the big market square at the front, there were spaces for more than 100 cars. Perfect.

I stayed at the hotel on the night before the seminar, as I always do, and came down in the morning all fired up and ready for the day ahead. Then I looked out of the window and my heart dropped to my shoes. It was market day. The dozens of car parking spaces on which I had previously counted were taken up with bustling market stalls and crowded with shoppers. All my seminar guests turned up and couldn't even get near the hotel. Indeed, they couldn't even find places to park in the surrounding streets. So what happened? They simply turned up, turned around and then drove home again. From that day on I always made sure that my team checked if there was a market on the day of our seminar, or anything else at all happening that could affect our attendance or cause a problem.

I've learned other lessons about my seminars along the way, too. For example, I never hold a seminar in a week with a bank holiday because so many people go away, especially if they are grandparents, who are often a prime audience for the products I am selling. Similarly, I always hold my seminars first thing in the morning, because I know that my elderly guests like to have a nap after lunch. You have to learn all of these lessons and keep learning them all the time. Over time you gradually get better and better.

I know that if I stick to the letter of my tried and tested strategy for seminars, I will always be successful. And I am.

One of my colleagues once came to me for advice on running a seminar and I very readily told him all that I knew. I am, as I have said many times, only too willing to share my experiences. Then, a week before the event, this colleague rang me up in a panic.

'No one is coming!' he shouted.

I ran through the checklist I had given him, step by step, and for a short while was baffled as to where it had gone wrong. However, when I asked him if he had sent out his invitations 28 days before the seminar, he revealed that he hadn't. There had been a problem and the mailing had only gone out ten days before the actual event.

Now, I know from experience and had expressly told him that the number one rule was always to send out the invitations 28 days before the event. If he couldn't do that, he shouldn't hold the seminar. It takes 28 days to get all the leads in and ten days is simply not enough time. No wonder no one had replied!

People always think they can take short cuts, or try something different. I can never understand it. If someone gives you the benefit of their hard-won experience, you should always take it. I gave this person the gift of my seminars on a plate and he completely screwed it up for the want of actually listening to simple instructions.

A desire to continually improve (and listen carefully to good advice) is what distinguishes a star salesperson and entrepreneur from an ordinary Joe Plonker. The ordinary Joe Plonker will sit back and wait until his company sends him on a course. Joe Plonker will sit there in their office for a set number of hours every day and relish the routine of a cup of coffee at ten o'clock and then again at three o'clock. Meanwhile, the true entrepreneur and star salesperson is doing everything they can to make a difference and using every single moment to get better. They are not going to wait to be told to do something.

If you have to be shown the way to do something, it is already too late. Chances are, your more fleet of foot and knowledge-hungry rivals have already done it.

100% of the 2%

I vividly remember Fred, a former colleague, who came into my office one day and told me he was on the brink of quitting the business. He had been struggling desperately and his sales record was dire. He said he had come to see me because I was a superstar and always had a perfect sales record. He asked, could I help him?

Naturally, I said I would do all that I could. But, on talking to him further, I rapidly came to the conclusion that actually he knew virtually nothing about the products we were selling. I asked him if he would mind waiting while I left my office for a few minutes and he hunched down into his chair, a veritable picture of despair.

I went straight to the stationery cupboard and got out a huge pile of all the brochures I could find on the financial products we were supposed to be selling, then walked back into the office and gave them to him. I said, in as gentle a manner as I could, that it would be a good idea to take them away and read them.

Fred's reaction was electric. He jumped out of his chair in a rage, picked up the brochures and threw them at me. He then stormed out of my office, giving me a mouthful of expletives and slamming the door behind him. I can still recall now how I felt while I watched the glass in the door shake and wondered if it was going to break.

Three or four months later, I was sitting in my office when Fred walked in.

Sensing my unease, he immediately said, 'Before you say anything, I am sorry. I am really, really sorry.'

He added that it was very important for him to tell me something. When he came to see me, he went on, he had all but decided to resign and thought that I was his last chance to stay in the industry. That morning, when I told him to go away and read the brochures, he thought I was simply being arrogant. I was, in his eyes, acting like a typical superstar who was unwilling to help the plebs down at the bottom end and that made him really angry. But, after he had left the office, he got to thinking that there might be something in reading all that stuff before he did actually resign. So he did. Then, just as I surmised, he was surprised by how much he didn't actually know and realised I was right.

The best thing about this story is it really did have a happy ending. The day before he came to apologise, he had just made his biggest ever sale and this had come on top of a growing successful streak. In fact, he had made more commission the day before than in the whole of the previous year. The lady whom he had been to see had had a very large sum of money to invest. After Fred had chatted with her for a short time she had said, 'You really seem to know what you are talking about; I have so much confidence in you that I would like you to look after all my investments.'

Fred recovered from his slump because he finally understood that to be a successful salesperson you need to know what it is that you are talking about. Most people who don't survive in our business don't survive because they don't know what it is that they are talking about. They pontificate and bluff and customers can see through them a mile off.

When you are involved in sales, there is a very basic rule that you would always do well to remember. That rule is that sales are 98% about people and 2% about product knowledge. But a good salesperson needs to know 100% of that 2% just in case they are asked.

The mistake that most people make is that once they have painstakingly learned that 100% they think they had darned well tell the poor client every little thing about the product to demonstrate their knowledge and flair. Regardless of whether that poor soul on the other end of this barrage wants to know it, or indeed is still listening at all. You don't need to demonstrate to the client that you know 100% of the 2%, just wait until you are asked and find out which particular part of the 2% that person wants to know. Instead, concentrate on the people side and personal skills and you will go far. If your would-be client sees that you are there for them, then it is a whole different story.

Sadly, most salespeople are hopeless at getting the balance right. I once went to a car showroom and thought for a bit of fun I would throw out buying signals to see if the salesman cottoned on and took the bait. I asked if they did this particular model in lime green. Was it possible to get leather upholstery? In purple? I wanted to see how he would react. But there was no sign that he could tell that I was really keen on the car.

I climbed inside and started asking about options for electric windows and the like. Again, he continued with his patter, and instead of answering my questions he insisted on opening the bonnet. Come and look at the engine, he entreated, clearly getting exasperated that I was not behaving exactly as I should.

I asked, 'Does it have an engine? If I put the key in here and turn it, will it go "vrrrm, vrrrm"? Will it get me from A to B?'

'Yes,' he said, looking confused.

'Young man,' I said, 'that is all I need to know.'

As it happened, in the end, I did buy a car from this poor chap. In fact we later became quite good friends and he confided in me that he had been very frustrated by my behaviour that day. However, when he later reflected on it, he realised that he had been getting too bogged down in the technicalities. He wanted to talk about horsepower, when I wanted to smell the leather. I tell that story often because most of the salespeople I have met spend too much time on the technical detail and not enough time on the individual that they are speaking to. There will always be some technophiles who want all the detail, but most won't. They want to know how the product will make them feel.

If you bombard people with too much technical detail, the prospect will only ever say they have too much to think about. Then they will walk away saying that they will come back to you and then go to see someone else who better understands their needs. All you will have done is warm them up for a competitor.

It happens to me all the time, I regularly see clients who have been warmed up by a bank and then fled to see me because I am not inundating them with unnecessary detail. Of course, in this circumstance, I am not complaining, but it is a salutary lesson to know your stuff well and to use it carefully too.

Pass it on

One year, while at the MDRT, someone was kind enough to say to me, 'John, you are a giant, a giant in the industry.'

I said, 'Thank you, that is very kind.' Then I thought of a quote I had previously heard and added, 'If I am a giant, it is because I stood on someone else's shoulders.'

It is true. I am what I am because I have learned from others. But I, in turn, am just as eager to pass this knowledge on.

This brings to mind the old story about the man who was bewailing God and saying, 'Where are you? Why are you not here with me, walking by my side?' Then God said, 'Look whose footprints are there.' The man looked down and saw that they were not his footprints; they were God's and God was carrying him. The man had never taken the time or trouble to look and see. You may say that this has nothing to do with selling, but it has everything to do with it. It is all to do with the inner self, which is what makes me different. Enthusiasm is the God within. When you have that passion about selling and it is bursting to get out of you, you sit down with people and they cannot help but be enthused with what you are getting enthused about. They pick up on those positive vibes. If anyone is prepared to listen, I will more than happily tell them all that I know.

A colleague at my company once asked me, how did I see myself? I was facetious enough to say, 'As a light shining in the darkness.' I said, and I really do believe it, that I can do more sales than anyone else because I put my marker in the sand. My marker in the sand is what I have learned from other people along the way. All I ever try to do is move the marker on.

If someone else can pass my marker I am delighted by that, because I never said, 'Here is my marker; you can't go past me.' I have always said, 'Here is my marker, and if you can go beyond it then I am thrilled.' If anyone learns something from me, that is the highest honour they could pay me.

Knowledge is power. Knowledge shared is power multiplied. I am always happy to share any knowledge I have. When you share and help someone up, someone else will help you up. If I have helped someone, the only thing I ask of them is to promise to help someone else. That is the only price I expect them to pay. If I help you and you help someone else, then we all get strengthened. We all move forward.

That is the principle of MDRT. We all share. We sit down with salespeople from all round the world and talk about what they do and how they do it. We are all richer in the knowledge. Once you have knowledge, who knows what you can achieve? The sky really is the limit.

Step Five: Belief

There are two types of belief I have always subscribed to; one is self-belief and the other is the belief of a life beyond. I've always been proud to have a strong Christian faith and this has been a very important part of both my and my wife's lives.

Religious faith is clearly a personal thing and I would not presume to preach to anyone how to live their life, but I would like to share how my own faith has helped me.

The advantage to having faith, whichever religion you subscribe to, is that if you believe there is something beyond where you are now, you are also aware that everything that you do today is going to be carried forward with you to wherever it is you go next. Therefore, it stands to reason that if you have got strong faith, you can't really ever be dishonest with your clients. It is simply not in you to be unethical with anyone and you can only really do the best for the people you deal with. It is the basic concept of having belief in something: you are ultimately answerable for your sins.

If you have faith your clients will see something different in you. They will see something in your eyes that shows that what you are saying comes from the heart.

I am never embarrassed to talk about my faith to my clients, if the situation warrants it. Many of my clients share my beliefs and, even if they are totally agnostic, people are always looking for someone they can trust. When you have that inner core of belief in someone or something else, that will inevitably come across really strongly to everyone you talk to and they will pick up on it very quickly. It helps them to relax and trust you. When someone can give you their trust, you have got them 100%.

If you have faith, true faith, you win people's respect. They see in you something different. They hear in you something different. They acknowledge in you something different. Most of the time that makes them very happy to deal with you. Occasionally they don't feel that way, but that is their prerogative. Everyone is entitled to their own opinions. I will add to that, on average, I make sales from at least eight out of ten of my appointments, which is not a bad hit rate. Whichever way you look at it, I am definitely doing something right.

The fact is, if you have faith, people feel it, they know it and you will be rewarded.

Ah, you may say, there is an ulterior motive in all your talk about belief and faith. You are only trying to get more business from clients. Well, I want to do business with my clients, yes, but that is not my starting point. It is actually more important for me to have a relationship with them first. If as a result of having that relationship I can do business with them, well, that is a nice bonus. Believe it or not, that business is a side issue. I wholeheartedly believe that all I do all day every day is go out to see people so we can interchange a few hours of our lives together. That, to me, is a very rewarding experience in itself. Any business on top of that is a bonus.

Perhaps this is different from the way that you expect a salesman to behave. The traditional notion is that salespeople put the pursuit of higher sales above all other considerations. Putting a relationship first may seem an anathema to many commission-hungry salespeople. However, think about it a different way. If I am different, maybe that is why I have been so successful. All successful salespeople have to have something that makes them different. For me, it has always been that core, that inner strength and resilience. When you have faith, what does it matter if you don't make a sale today? What does it matter if something went wrong today? What matters is that there is something further on down the line, and what happens today or tomorrow is just transitory. Faith doesn't just help me survive; it underpins everything else I have been talking about in this book, from my positive mental attitude to my constant quest to educate and improve myself.

Faith has also equipped me with a very strong self-belief which has been vital in helping me meet my goals. I will talk about goals in more detail later in this book, but suffice it to say here that, as a salesperson, you should always give yourself goals.

My self-belief has been an important factor in meeting my goals. I know that it has got me to where I am today because I believed and dreamed all those years ago that I would be where I am. It is no surprise to me that I have achieved what I have and got as far as I have, because I planned it all along.

You don't have to set yourself big goals to start with. Remember, though: if you have a big dream you tend to achieve a big result. So dream the dream. Set a goal and believe that you can get there. If you do, you will.

The way it works is simple. You have the vision and then you have the dream. Then you set the plan to realise that dream and you work the plan. It is that easy. My vision for the past decade has been to be my company's all-time number one revenue-producing partner. I dream about it every day and constantly visualise myself standing at the podium at the firm's annual get together at auspicious locations such as the Royal Albert Hall in London. In my mind's eye I can see the chairman shaking my hand and congratulating me for being the best salesperson yet again. It is therefore, to me, no coincidence that I have indeed been up on stage every year but one for the past 18 years, being lauded for my achievements. I believed it would happen and it did.

Having these dreams and believing you can do it motivates you to get out there every day and make it happen.

I am not embarrassed about my faith or dreams. I never try to hide them. I have always been totally open about my sales targets and my goals. Again, though, I find myself in the minority compared to my fellow salespeople. Most of them, if they have bothered to set targets and goals, like to keep them a closely guarded secret just in case they don't achieve them. They believe that if they haven't told anyone, no one will ever know that they have failed and they won't lose face among their peers.

My view is: tell everyone. When a target is public knowledge it is much more difficult to explain why you haven't done what you said you were going to do. If you believe in it, shout it from the rooftops. If it is a genuine belief, you know it will happen anyway.

Believe in your clients

One Saturday morning, about 35 years ago, I met a prospective client in his timber yard. The business was small and, at that time, he employed just two people and he was doing a lot of the manual labour himself. That day, when I first met him, he was busy sawing two bits of wood as I arrived. When he eventually downed his tools and we started chatting, it emerged that he didn't have much money but was minded to invest what he had. Eventually, I sold him a £10 per month savings plan. Mind you, I had to work hard to make that sale, but after a fair bit of banter we shook hands on the deal.

I, of course, kept in touch, and I watched with a mix of pleasure and fascination as this hard-working entrepreneur built up his business. In what seemed like no time, he was suddenly employing 200 people and was selling his wares to a wider and wider network of customers. It seemed like nothing could stop him.

One day he called me and said, 'John, I like your style. I need pensions for all these people; come and sort it all out for me.'

So I did.

Then a little later he called again and said, 'I now have all these directors. Is it possible to sort them out an executive pension scheme?'

So I sorted that out too.

Then, a few years later, his company got taken over by a larger business and my client went straight onto the main board of the company that had bought him out. Sure enough, not much later, I got a phone call asking me to sort out the executive pension scheme at the larger firm, because my entrepreneurial friend had discovered that the existing scheme was in a complete mess. I did that too. Eventually, and I could hardly believe it myself, the larger company got taken over too and this time my super-successful client became chairman of a prestigious national group. Once again, he called me in and this time I was asked to sort out millions of pounds of pension business.

Goodness knows how much business I eventually did on the back of that little £10 savings scheme. I lost count after a while. To me, though, the moral of that story is: if you don't believe in all your clients and do not look after those small clients, which was in this case the buyer of a £10 per month savings plan, you won't get the multi-million pounds' worth of business I eventually got.

I never, ever worry about being cost efficient. I take each client as they come and know that even if they invest a small amount today, if I treat them well, they will probably come back and do more tomorrow, or may refer me on elsewhere where I will pick up other business. It all comes back to having faith and self-belief. My own personal belief is that the man upstairs arranges this in his wisdom. You may think differently. Either way, you should always have faith that from little acorns, big oaks do grow, because they invariably do if you look after them properly.

When I go to see someone, I never concern myself about how much I will make from that particular appointment. That would be distracting and self-defeating. My statistics tell me every time I see someone, whether I sell to them or not, what my average earnings are. If I have ten appointments, I know what my earnings will be this week based on this average. Similarly, if I have 20 appointments in a month, I know what my earnings will be based on this average. That is what my records tell me and, to be honest, that is all I need to know. I might make this money from one of the appointments, or across all 20 of them, or via several of them in the middle. It doesn't matter. It would be completely wrong to look at the cost of doing business from the perspective that every appointment has to generate X thousand pounds. That is looking at it from completely the wrong angle. A successful salesperson looks at every meeting on its merits and has faith that it is the right thing to do. Do that and the rest will follow.

One of my longest-serving clients was a lovely lady called Mrs Brody. I met her and her husband early in my career and liked them enormously. Even though they were in their seventies when we first met, they were very active. They kept horses and rode them regularly. Sadly, Mr Brody died suddenly in his early eighties and his dear wife started to go blind. They had only ever made small investments, but my heart went out to her because she had no relatives nearby to care for her. I said to Cathy, my PA, that if ever I was in Dunstable where Mrs Brody lived, I must always call in to see her, even if I only had half an hour to spare. I'd go as regularly as I could and pop in for a cup of tea, a biscuit and a nice chat. Sometimes it was only a couple of times a year, but I knew it made a big difference to her. Eventually, she too passed away. Soon after, her son came to see me and said he wanted to meet me because his mother had spoken so much about me. She knew that she was one of my smallest clients, and she probably was, but it had made a real difference that I had always looked after her and made the effort to keep in touch. The son said that, when they got the estate sorted out, he would like to talk to me. I said fine and thanked him for looking me up but thought little of it after that. A year later he came to see me and said he had it all sorted out. He had sold the house and told me that he had £150,000 from Mrs Brody's estate that he wanted me to invest for him. Just like that.

I had no reason to know that he would ever do that and, indeed, never even considered it when I was visiting his mother. The fact is, though, if you look after the Mrs Brodys of this world, the chances are a few years later someone like her son will come along and invest a substantial sum with you. There are no guarantees, but I have always found that if you look after your clients and you do genuinely care about them, they will care about you. Your faith will always be repaid. If you treat people in an honest and fair way and you treat them all the same whatever their status, then you will never lose business.

As I said earlier, one of the greatest things you can learn as a salesperson is, if you get it right, from the smallest acorns the mightiest oaks truly do grow. But you can never judge which acorn will grow into an oak tree. Many people in sales think you can. They think, oh, this is going to be a big one, so I will give this person special attention and look after them more than I will my other clients. I've even heard people grade their clients on a sliding scale from, say, A to F or 1 to 7. They are quick to dismiss anyone that doesn't immediately look promising and clearly can't be bothered with grade D, E or F clients. In my experience, though, it is those much-vaunted A- and B-list potential clients that often end up falling on stony ground. While these short-sighted salespeople concentrate on chasing these ultimately worthless dreams, they will have blindly thrown away the precious D, E and F clients which in all likelihood would have turned out to be the ones to gradually grow to mighty oaks. If only these impatient salespeople had been patient and sensible and kept the faith, they could have grown with them, too.

Believe in the product

If you came round to my house today, tomorrow, next month or next year, I guarantee that you would be offered a McVitie's biscuit with your tea or coffee. Even though I worked for the firm more than 40 years ago, I still feel so passionately about their products that I cannot abide another brand of biscuit in the house. McVitie's make the best biscuits and there is nothing that you or anyone else can say that will persuade me to change my mind on that.

If you sell a product, you have to believe that that product is the best. I do, whether I am selling biscuits, calculating machines or financial products, and I would if I were selling cars or cartwheels too! I always put my money where my mouth is, too. At this moment in time, I probably carry more life assurance than anyone else I have ever met. In fact, my company once sent me a list of my top life assurance clients; I was number one and Sherry, my wife, was number two. Even I had to laugh. But there is a serious point here. Why shouldn't I invest in the products I sell every day? How can I go to someone else and tell them to pay £10,000 for a life insurance policy if I won't buy it ten times over myself?

Clients often ask me, do you have these investments? I say, yes, I do.

'If they are good enough for me and mine, they are good enough for you and yours,' I can say with all honesty.

If someone doesn't believe in their product, it stands out a mile. It is actually very off-putting for those on the other side, too. I once got in a taxi and from the moment I got in the driver was effing and blinding and was very aggressive. I was a bit taken aback, not least because I don't really like swearing. So I waited for him to draw breath and said, 'Are you all right?'

'No,' he said. 'I hate this effing job.'

I said, 'For goodness' sake, how many years have you been a taxi driver?'

'Sixteen years,' he said with a sad shake of his head.

'Why don't you give it up and do something you like doing?' I asked.

He looked at me as though I had just asked him to drive me to the moon. At long last he sighed and said that he had very few options open to him. Apart from that, he added, he couldn't be bothered to look elsewhere because everything else would be just as bad.

Summoning up the courage and fully expecting another barrage of abuse, I advised the man to consider other options, or he would more than likely have a heart attack and drop dead.

'Get out from under,' I advised. 'If you are doing a job you hate, you are dead in the water. Dead in the water. You are not being fair to yourself; more importantly, you are not being fair to the clients.'

He was so consumed with anger and bitterness that he probably dismissed me as an interfering busybody. I could see my advice fell on deaf ears and dread to think what happened to him. However, there is a lesson to be learned here. If you are selling something or offering a service that makes you think, actually, this is a bit of a con really, but I'll flog it anyhow, you won't be able to do it with any degree of success. The same goes for when your heart just isn't in it. You have to be able to step out of your front door brimming with self-confidence and 100% belief in the product you sell. It has to be part of your DNA. It always has been for me, which is why my biscuit tin knows no other product than McVitie's and absolutely never will.

It is very easy for a salesperson keen to make a sale and to put bread and butter on the table to 'exaggerate' a bit about the benefits of a product. Pressure can make any man desperate, but lying is not the answer. Apart from anything else, if someone is desperate, it becomes immediately apparent to clients. It will make the prospect feel nervous and unsure, which is clearly not the best atmosphere in which to make a sale.

The only way you will make consistently good sales is if you are open, honest and have belief in the product. Your passion and powers of persuasion will shine through and everyone will feel relaxed, comfortable and in the mood to spend money. Better still, you'll find that you don't need to put the pressure on after all because people will trust what you say. It is amazing what will happen to you if you understand and learn this simple lesson.

People say it is OK for me because I'm working from a position of consistent and long-standing success, but it wasn't always like that. I had to start from somewhere. However, from the start I understood that if I was straight, honest and ethical, and all of the things that I have talked about here, people would see something different in me. They would see in me someone they wanted to deal with, and usually I would make the sale as a consequence. It was that straightforward.

Plus, by doing this, I have given myself a great feeling inside. To be able to go out there and make people feel better because they spoke to you is a fantastic gift. Knowing you have inspired someone is an amazing experience.

Every single day when I get home in the evening I ask myself the following questions. What have I done to improve my wealth today? What have I done to improve my life today? What have I done to improve myself as a person today? Have I done something that I am proud of, or something that I am ashamed of? I like to think it is always something I am proud of, because that is what it is all about and where true success lies.

Leave the ego at home

One of the greatest tragedies about salespeople is that, as things start looking up and they become successful, far too many become arrogant. Overnight they will suddenly stop dealing with people whom they perceive to be 'less important' than them. They appear to lose all sense of what is right or wrong and are rude and brusque to everyone around them. Worst of all, they just don't seem to know how to control their ego, yet can't seem to comprehend that if it is not kept in check it could destroy them at work and at home. When I see this happening among my colleagues I often say to them, being number one in your company can never, ever be as important as being number one in your home with your wife and children. Most of the time, though, people have no idea what I am talking about because they are probably too far down the path of greed and over-arching ambition.

I do, however, speak from experience. Before I joined my present company, I was with my previous company for 18 years. At this company, if you were one of the top 35 earners out of 5,000 people you were entitled to the title 'president'. If you were a president, then you couldn't help but feel that you were really someone. At the end of the year you would step up on stage at the annual conference and be lauded by all your peers. Everyone wanted to be made president because everyone would be saying what a great guy or girl they were and they would get all the trappings of being a superstar. I was proud to achieve this status in my third year.

Unfortunately, in my fourth year I really struggled and by the end of the year I had not done enough to make president for that period. I was gutted. When I went to the annual conference my ego was so deeply dented that I nearly jumped off the balcony in shame. I couldn't bear to watch the other successful presidents getting all the praise. I was determined that this would not happen to me again and that next year I would be back up on that stage, by hook or by crook.

After working my fingers to the bone throughout the year I made president once again. I rushed home to tell Sherry the news and said triumphantly, 'I made it!' My sales figures had reached the magical £100,000 and I was destined for that stage once more.

Sherry turned to me with a completely straight face and said, 'Good, I hope you are happy.'

This was not the reaction I had expected at all. I could see she was very cross.

'What is the matter?' I asked.

She replied, 'You've been an absolute ******* to live with these last 12 months. You've been so goal orientated and driven by your ego that you have completely lost sight of me and the kids. I don't ever want you to be like you've been again.'

My wife doesn't swear. In 46 years of marriage she has only sworn twice, and this was one of those occasions. I was really hurt when she said it, but I also quickly realised that she was right. I promised her there and then that I would never be like that again, and I hope that I never have.

If you do not keep a careful check on your ego, you will become bloated by your own achievements. You will be sucked into the myth that all that matters is your own success and personal elevation. This manifests itself in some truly horrible qualities. People like this never care who they offend, or trample over, to get what they want. Every company has people like this. They'll pick up the phone and yell at people until they get what they want. They'll even do it to their spouses and don't seem to care who is listening. They have no respect for anyone at any level. Somehow they equate success with rudeness and arrogance.

Many years ago I worked with a hugely successful director who rose swiftly through the ranks from being a manager to a regional manager, to regional director and then to a board director. His progress was breathtaking to watch and everyone around admired him. But do you know what? Despite all his success, every night he went home to an empty house. He had driven his wife and children away with his single-minded, ruthless ambition. I kept wondering, what was it all for?

Whenever people start believing their own PR, that is when it all starts to fall apart. Of course, they will blame the wife, or the kids, or the environment, or the stress of the job. They will never for a moment consider that it is their own bloody-mindedness that has driven away everything they hold dear.

I heard another great example of this from a friend in America. He told me about a father who never went to see his kid's school sports matches. When his son got into the junior baseball team, this man said, 'Son, I am so proud of you. I will come to see you play on Friday.' But somehow, when Friday came around, he was too busy and didn't get there.

Then his son got into the high school team and he said the same thing: 'Son, I am so proud of you. I will be there to see you play on Friday.' Again, he didn't make it.

A few years later, his son got into the state team and once more this chap said, 'Son, I am so proud of you and will come to see you.'

This time, he managed to get there. He proudly went up to his son and said, 'I am here! I am here!'

The son, who was 17 years old by now, said, 'Nice to see you, Dad; where have you been for the last 17 years?

He then turned his back on his father and walked away. The father realised he had lost his son that day. Indeed, he had probably lost him forever. It would never, ever be the same between them. He had paid a high price because his ego had been so strong that he had believed he had to be in the office every Friday afternoon and therefore hadn't got to any of his son's matches. He should have been there, not in the office.

It does not matter if you have ambitions to be the highest ever grossing salesperson. You have to realise what really matters in life. For me family has always been number one and since I learned my lesson I have always put them first. One of my great personal claims to fame is I have never ever missed a school speech day, sports day or nativity play. I was always there for my wife and children because I believed it was far more important than going out to see clients.

It is equally important to always be as polite and personable as humanly possible to everyone around me at work, both colleagues and clients. It is a personal rule of mine to always say 'please' and 'thank you' and to always turn up on time to meetings. I am especially nice to people who answer the phones, as everyone else seems to believe they have carte blanche to treat them like dirt.

I also pay close attention to my image; I always dress smartly, wearing a tie and matching handkerchief every day, and would not dream of leaving the house without polishing my shoes. I believe that it makes people around me comfortable because they see someone who looks like a professional. I wouldn't dream of turning up in my shirt sleeves, even on a hot summer day, yet I am amazed by how many salespeople do. They even wear jeans or trendy jackets, which to me gives off completely the wrong signals. I don't believe salespeople should look like their clients; it starts everything off on the wrong footing.

None of these things cost me anything but time and a bit of shoe polish. When I first started as a salesman, I couldn't afford to have the number of suits I have today, but every night when I got home I used to press my trousers and make sure that I would look good the following morning.

I passionately believe that all this makes a massive difference to the people around me and makes a huge difference to me too. I am putting the needs and sensibilities of others first and that is how it should be.

This combination of smart dress with a polite and upbeat attitude should be reflected in everything you do – even when other people do not make it easy.

When I left one of my former companies, they were really unpleasant about it. I was one of their top performing salesmen and had quite a high profile in the firm, so they tried to make an example of me. While I utterly understand the point of stopping salespeople from taking their clients with them, I remember feeling quite shocked by their behaviour, which went far beyond the usual contractual obligations. However, one of the things I have learned is not to be bitter and never to run with hate in your heart. If you run with hate in your heart it will only destroy you. So I put it to one side, said a polite farewell and got on with my new job.

A few months down the line, one of my former clients phoned the firm I had left and asked to speak to the salesman who had taken over my accounts from me. He asked if it would be possible for this chap to arrange a visit to his home in Southend. After the barest minimum of pleasantries, the first question my replacement asked was: are you going to do any more business? My poor former client said no, but he would (quite properly) like to meet the person who was dealing with all his investments. Unbelievably, the salesperson snorted with derision and refused. He said there was no way he would be driving from his office in Northampton to Southend if there was no business at the end of it. If this person wanted to see him that much he would have to pay his travelling expenses.

My former client was as shocked as I was at the behaviour of this firm. He managed to stammer out 'but John Cross always came to see me' before the conversation was abruptly terminated. He then got in touch with me and, very properly, I told him that, while I very much appreciated his getting in touch, I was sadly unable to deal with him for the time being because I had signed a non-competitive document. He was very understanding, if not altogether happy with his situation. However, I did discover from our conversation that all he really wanted was an update on his investments, so I rang my old firm and made sure he was sent one. I felt saddened by the episode, but pushed it to the back of my mind.

Two years later, my old client got in touch again and by now I was free to do business with him. He said, 'John, do you remember I told you about a little company I had? Well, someone has bought it for £800,000.'

'Congratulations,' I said, genuinely pleased for him.

'Thank you,' he said. Then he added, 'The reason for my call is I would like to invest it all through you. I appreciated that even though you couldn't deal with me after you left your previous company, you still took the time and trouble to make sure that my requirements were met by contacting your previous company on my behalf.'

I had no idea that all those visits to him in Southend in my past would bear fruit like this. But they did. The crazy thing is, though, if my successor at the other firm had swallowed his pride and gone out of his way, he could have easily picked up this business. He had plenty of time to woo this client.

It just goes to show that a little humility, faith and politeness can go a very long way indeed.

Step Six: Honesty and trust

Over the years I have learned that if you ask a question in the right way, people will always give you the answer you want. I got my first experience of just how effective this can be in my early days as a salesman for McVitie and Price. One of the first things my superiors at the biscuit firm told me was: get the client's confidence and trust. Once you had won that confidence and trust you will be able to ask for anything, they said. I was a little perplexed at first as to what they meant. What should I be asking from these clients? I pondered. After all, wasn't I supposed to be selling to them?

After further enquiry, it turned out the 'ask' was whether I, the McVitie and Price representative, could check inside their stock room.

I can't tell you what a powerful thing this could be. Once you had gained the confidence of a client, you could brightly say, 'Is it OK to pop out back and check your stock?'

'No problem,' they'd say, with a wave of their hands. 'Help yourself.'

I'd then stride confidently through the shop and into their stock rooms, which were invariably stacked high with boxes of everything from tins of soup to rows of kitchen towels. But I would hardly notice all these grocery paraphernalia because I would be there to see how many packets of biscuits they had left. I'd carefully count how many boxes of Penguins, digestives and custard creams there were. Then I'd pop back into the shop and say, 'I've just had a quick look and you need some more digestives, custard creams and ginger nuts.'

'Right, then,' the shopkeeper would reply. 'You had better order them up.'

After that it would be plain sailing. I could easily say, well, that is four boxes, but if you order five boxes you'll get a 5%

63

discount. They'd say OK and I would have made a sale. It is astonishing how easy it was.

There was, however, one golden rule to all this, and that was: you never ripped anyone off. We all knew that if we did that once and told someone they needed to order a bunch of custard creams when they didn't really need any, we would never set foot into that stock room again. The confidence and trust would have been shattered. Those shopkeepers were a canny bunch and did not take kindly to anyone seeking to make a fast buck by abusing their trust. And quite rightly so.

Back in those days, McVitie's were unique in their approach. As far as I know, no other salesmen ever imagined they could waltz into a stock room and practically fill in their own order book. Believe it or not, we even did this with grocery giants like Tesco, although they were a lot smaller back at that time. I clearly remember going into the massive stockroom of my local Tesco store and chatting to the manager afterwards. Then, while I was telling him that he needed 20 boxes of digestives, 15 boxes of custard creams and ten boxes of so and so, I said, 'I notice you've got Crawford's biscuits, but ours are a lot nicer.'

The Tesco manager said, 'OK, let's try yours for a change.'

Then I even took it a bit further. I told him that the biscuits would be delivered on Thursday, but he needn't worry his staff with it, because when they were delivered I would go in and put them out on the shelves for him. When I went back in to set the biscuits out I went to town on a big display and everyone was delighted. It wouldn't happen now, of course, with the massive centralised distribution systems, but the principle of trust is something no salesperson should ever forget, no matter what you are selling.

A little understanding of the importance of trust can take you a long way. Indeed, McVitie and Price became so powerful by working so closely in harmony with their clients that they eventually took over their main competitors, including Crawford's and McDonald, to form the multi-billion pound turnover confectionery giant United Biscuits. Not a bad return for all those trips into stockrooms.

Of course, my job is a little different today. I am no longer selling commodities like biscuits. I am selling concepts. With commodities, it is easy for a customer to quickly ascertain the taste, colour and texture of the product and make a judgment about whether the product represents value for money. With concepts like financial services, that is not so easy. Things are much more abstract and it is a more difficult sell because I cannot show a client what the product looks like. I cannot physically show what they will get from their investment, other than by producing graphs and diagrams. But even then these are just representations, not a solid product that you can touch, smell or see.

This is why honesty, integrity and trust are even more important in my career today and why they should be important to you whatever you are selling. If a client has confidence in what you are saying, they will feel comfortable and open to the prospect of working with you and buying your product even if they can't physically see it. Indeed, if you get the trust and honesty part sorted out, you won't need to make the sale at all. The client will make the sale for you.

I have always said, 'I never "make a sale"; the client always buys.' It is true. I just take lots of orders! All I have had to do is inspire trust in my clients though being honest, consistent and true to my word. Once anyone does that, it will be plain sailing afterwards.

Never lie

Trust and honesty are the two key motivators in sales. They create the basis for a lifelong relationship and should be every salesperson's calling card. Get that right and you've got it cracked. Once you are trusted and have earned a reputation for being an honest person, people will do almost anything for you.

Far too many people think exaggeration, even lying, will help them get a sale. They feel obliged to 'talk up' a product well beyond its innate qualities. Let me say now, it won't help make a sale. Indeed, apart from anything else, if you are a liar you have to have a very good memory because you have to remember the lies you told every time you see your prospect. I wouldn't be able to do that; in fact most people can't, which is why liars always slip up. The best salespeople always tell the whole truth straight away to ensure there are no misunderstandings later on. Customers hate unpleasant surprises.

If you always tell the truth you needn't worry about what you say in the future. I always say to people at my seminars that I said the same thing to clients ten years ago that I say today. If I am lying, at least my lies are consistent! Joking aside, a good salesperson has to be dead straight and dead honest. Always.

There is no shame in not knowing something. There is only shame in not being straight and honest. If my clients ask me something that I don't know, I do everything I can to find the answer to their question as quickly and efficiently as possible. No one minds waiting a short while, particularly if the information they subsequently get is well considered and correct. I'm quite open about the fact that I don't immediately know the answer and will say, 'Do you mind if I call the office and check that?' I will also thank them because their question has helped me learn something new.

Many salespeople won't do that. They see telling a client that they don't know something as a weakness. They'd rather lie to save face, when really they are doing exactly the opposite. When a client finds out that they are bullshitting, and they will, they will be so disappointed that the bond of trust will be shattered forever.

Oh, it is OK for you, you might say, you are just so enthusiastic about everything. Sometimes you do have to exaggerate, even if it is only a little, just to get a client interested, you might add. Do you know what I say to that? You don't need to lie or bullshit if you are just so excited about what you are selling that you are bursting to tell everyone all about it.

If you want to be enthusiastic, do all the things I have been talking about in this book. Learn about your product; get to know it inside out and upside down. Then show your enthusiasm to the world. Don't hide it. Anyone can do this, and when they do there is no point in resorting to lies.

It all goes back to truly believing in the products you sell. You can't be enthusiastic about something you don't believe in. There is a name for people who fake this enthusiasm. They are called con merchants. They pretend to be enthusiastic about something to gain advantage. If you don't believe passionately that the company you are working for is the right company and has the right products, and you don't believe passionately that you are doing your clients a favour when you persuade them to buy this particular product, you have no right to be out there doing your job. You are out there for all the wrong reasons. All you are thinking about is your own advantage, not the advantage of the client.

People often say to me, 'How do I know I can trust you?' I always tell them to look into my eyes and see into my heart. My honesty is not a cynical act; it really does come from my heart. If my prospects feel comfortable with what they can see there, then they can trust me. If they don't, they won't and they need to deal with someone else. It is entirely their choice. The problem is that, over time, most people do become guarded and wary. They've been ripped off and lied to too often by unscrupulous salespeople. I hope, though, that people can see in me something that is different from most other salesmen that they have dealt with and that helps them to relax.

One of the things I say to all of my new clients is, 'Trust me: you need me, you need my help and you need my advice. If you give me your trust, I will not let you down. I will be here for you when you want to see me.' Then I make sure that I do just that.

Lying, of course, takes many forms, from out-and-out fibs about a product or service on offer to covering up when you've made a mistake.

We all make mistakes. None of us is perfect. If I make a mistake, or anyone at my office in Royston screws up, the number one rule is that we tell the clients straight away. Then we apologise and put it right. It is usually something pretty petty, like someone keying in the wrong account number or bank details. But the fact that it can be easily corrected does not undermine its significance to the client. The only correct thing to do is put your hands up, agree you've made a howler, say sorry and put it right.

Even if you are this honest and straightforward, it does not follow that clients will always reciprocate and indeed, in my experience, more often than not they like to vent a little steam.

Thankfully, it is very rare that mistakes are made at my office, but I have, on some occasions over the years, found my team in tears. Sometimes it is as a result of a misunderstanding. Other times it is down to a client who is furious at a presumed slight, or simply won't accept an apology over something which has not quite gone as expected. If a client is being totally unreasonable, I will turn the tables a little, because it is not fair to take things out on my hard-working, dedicated office staff. However, I will keep it as light-hearted as possible, particularly if we have been at fault.

I once had a client on the phone who was screaming and shouting over something that had not gone quite as smoothly as any of us might have hoped. The problem had, however, been discovered quickly and then corrected. He had spent some time expressing his displeasure to my team and now it was my turn. I let this client vent his spleen for a while and then asked him to hold on for just a moment. I called to Cathy, my PA, and asked her to come into the office. I knew the gentleman on the other end of the phone could hear every word as I said, 'Cathy, I have Mr X on the phone and he is very upset, as you know. Can you get your hat and coat, because you are fired.'

Cathy was in on the ruse and, raising her voice a little to ensure she was heard on the other end of the phone, she thanked me, said she was sorry but understood my position was untenable and wished me well. She then walked out of my office and gave the door a theatrical slam for good measure.

By now, the poor client on the other end of the phone was beside himself and feeling very sober and remorseful indeed. He managed to splutter out, 'Why did you do that?' I feigned complete surprise and said that I thought that was what he wanted.

To cut a long story short, my little drama exercise completely deflated his bubble of anger and calmed the situation down. Needless to say, Cathy received a bouquet and a box of chocolates from this man a few days later and hopefully he never again took out his anger on innocent office staff.

It is not good to make mistakes, but, as we all know, they do happen. It is up to you to make people understand that if you make a mistake you will always admit it and will put it right immediately. If they then lose their temper and shout at people on your team, particularly those who are not particularly in a position to defend themselves, then the injured party is now in the wrong.

If you have a good relationship and are only ever open and honest, your dealings with clients will always turn out well in the end.

No one likes being 'sold to'

If you know that you are being honest, it will mean that you automatically relax and this will be reflected in everything you do and say. Better still, it will put your clients at ease.

This knowledge worked particularly well for me when I was dealing with a particularly difficult customer at one time. He constantly chopped and changed, pontificated and mumbled and kept drifting away from the point. After a short while into yet another inconclusive meeting with this fellow, I mentally gave up and sat back in my chair. He immediately noticed this and said, 'You seem very relaxed about this.'

I replied that it was not my intention to twist his arm and make him do something he didn't want to do or did not feel comfortable with. I added that I thought that the product I had been discussing was right for him and met his goals perfectly, but if he didn't feel ready to do anything, then that was completely his choice. Then I smiled and said, 'Please don't worry about my side of things; I hit my annual sales target last week, so I am completely relaxed.'

This poor chap sat bolt upright in his chair and exclaimed, 'You hit your annual sales targets last week? But it is only the beginning of October!'

Now he was listening. It turned out he had done some selling himself in the past and knew that hitting your annual targets a full three months ahead of schedule was a pretty impressive feat. Before I knew it he was striding across the room to fetch his cheque book and asking which name he would make the payment to for his investment.

The moment he realised that I was there for him, not for me, he was happy to give me the cheque. That is the key to successful selling. If your clients see that you are completely straight with them and are considering their interests above your own, they will automatically relax too. Any anxieties they have about being 'sold to' disappear.

People don't just buy products, services or ideas. They buy how they imagine they will *feel* when they use them. It stands to reason that they want to feel good about what they buy. Your job as a salesperson is to help them feel good, and if they feel hectored, or that you are just in it for yourself, then the shutters go up and they become hostile and unsure.

Imagine yourself on the other side. Most of us start off in a position of automatically distrusting the person who is trying to sell us something, particularly if they seem to be trying just a bit too hard. Maybe you've had a bad experience in the past and have known the disappointment of feeling let down or ripped off. Or maybe you've just heard 'bad things' about the industry. But, if someone can persuade you through their relaxed and open manner that they will not let you down and you can always count on them for good service and support if it is ever needed, half the battle is won. Trust is the unwritten contract between you.

Never forget that the person whom salespeople like to label with the impersonal moniker of 'client', or 'prospect', or 'lead', is actually still a person. In fact, first and foremost, they are a person. Once you start treating them as a commodity, or a sales statistic, or as something towards your annual target, you reduce yourself to the position of being a peddler of goods. To me, even the word 'peddler' doesn't sound very nice and, believe me, it is not very nice for the person on the other end of the patter.

If you ever find yourself only concerned about getting what you want out of a deal, rather than thinking about what the poor soul at the other end of your entreaties actually needs, the trust part of the relationship goes out of the window.

It is for this reason that I always ensure that it is me personally who goes to see my clients, no matter whether they just want a catch-up or have thousands of pounds to invest. Yes, I have an office full of highly capable support staff who help me in all manner of ways, and some pretty savvy sales colleagues too, but I have never wanted to delegate seeing my clients. I strongly believe that if you want a relationship based on honesty and trust, you have to put in the legwork yourself, and that means getting out there and being seen.

I once went to see a client in Suffolk and I could tell from the moment that I arrived that something was troubling her. I'd been there for half an hour talking about an ISA transfer of £10,000 when she finally came out with it.

Looking straight at me, she said, 'Do you mind if I ask you something?'

I assured her with a smile that I always welcomed any questions.

'Why have you come to see me?' she asked.

'Well, I came here because you asked for a meeting,' I said, wondering where this might be leading.

She clearly wasn't satisfied with my answer and pressed her case again. 'No, why have *you* come to see me?' she said.

I was by now thoroughly confused and could only say, 'Well, why wouldn't I?'

Then we got to the crux of the matter. This lady told me that she knew that I was one of the top salesmen at my company and was obviously a busy man. Her question to me was, how could I afford the time to come and see her? Why wasn't I sending along a minion to take her details and arrange the relatively straightforward ISA transfer? She would have thought that perfectly normal and indeed had not really expected me to turn up that day at all.

Now I understood. My reply was simple, honest and to the point.

I said, 'I am a very successful salesman, but it is because I come and see people like you that I am successful. I care about my clients, and it is important to me that I am always there to see them and give them the fullest and best possible service.'

I could see from the broad smile on her face that she both understood and fully approved.

A good salesman should focus on making someone's life better. I don't just mean just with the initial sale, but month in and month out after that. It will make all the difference. Anyone can talk a great game. It is what you do after that talk, after the promises have been made, that makes all the difference.

Don't always go for the 'big' sale

I have long held a reputation in my firm for making more sales than anyone else, but when I first meet a client I never set out to take every penny they have. That is not the way to build trust. Apart from anything else, it can be utterly self-defeating, because if you push some people too hard, too quickly, they may well take fright and walk away for good. If a client has £10, I am perfectly happy to take £1 when we first meet and then go back for the other £9 at a later date. I know my patience will be rewarded.

Of course, if someone is prepared to invest £100,000 straight away, I will obviously go straight for the full amount, but if they are not, I am more than prepared to play the long game. It is all a question of judgment. With experience and patience, though, anyone can learn to work out whether the person they are speaking to wants to do something big right now or would prefer to take things a bit slower.

If a person is nervous, or scared to commit, I have no problem at all with taking things at a slower place. I will reassure them and ask them if perhaps they'd like to come along to another seminar before we go any further. A second visit to one of my seminars often helps soothe any anxieties. That's fine by me. You should never be afraid to play the long game. I am in no tearing hurry. You cannot move forward in sales until you establish trust. Once you establish trust you have got them forever.

I have often found that people will come up to me after their second or even third seminar and say that they are now ready to do something. They will add that they now understand so much more than last time and, because I have not been pushy or overbearing, they can see that I am a straight shooter and will give me more money as a result.

Even then, I am more than happy to invest half of their money and come back at a later date for more. But, rest assured, I will always go back for the other half. As a matter of strict routine, I always write to clients immediately after our first meeting and confirm that I will be back in six months for a review, just as I said at the meeting. I then make sure that they are called six months later to the day of my saying I would be back in touch. I will have that review, show my client that their investment did everything I promised it would do and then ask if they feel confident to invest the rest. Handle it like this and they usually do. I have done everything that I said I would do and kept my word to the letter. After all, the next sale you make is based on the success of the last one.

There is always a danger that if you leave it for three or six months for someone to 'think about' it, they will do anything but. Things come up every day which distract us and if something is on the back burner it can often slip a long way down our list of priorities, so much so that it can be forgotten forever. In three or six months' time they will be in exactly the same position as before. We are all a little bit guilty of this. However, if I do what I said I would do, i.e. get back in touch in three or six months' time, there is no danger of our discussions slipping off the agenda completely. Plus, as people get to know me, they will understand that I am a man of my word. They know that they had better give it some thought because I will always get back in touch on the day I said I would.

I am careful, though, never, ever to force anyone into a corner. As I said earlier, my mantra is 'never be afraid to take the pound on the table, and go back for the £9 later on'. I have learned to do that. In my experience you will always get the full sale in the end.

Some of my biggest clients today started off as my smallest clients all those years ago. Believe me, the basis of sales is about caring for people, and if you care about anyone you don't just want a short-term relationship, which is unsatisfactory for both sides. That is no good to anyone. You want a deep, long-term association that is to your mutual benefit.

My constant wish is that people always be left feeling really pleased that they have dealt with me. I could not be happier if, as I get up to leave, I hear my clients say they are glad that I am looking after their financial affairs.

Plus, don't forget, if one client feels this way, they will almost certainly tell other people about this amazing financial expert they know. As everyone knows, a word-of-mouth referral is more powerful than many thousands of pounds' worth of advertising and I have long since lost count of the amount of business I have picked up from recommendations from satisfied clients.

Even if it is not referral business, I am always more than happy to let existing clients talk to potential clients too. I've got nothing to hide and trust my clients as much as I hope they trust me. I know how reassuring this sort of reference can be to new clients, so why wouldn't I encourage it to happen?

Treat people how you would like to be treated yourself

In my early days as a salesman I used to make between 50 and 100 calls a day to drum up meetings. After a period of time I thought, hold on, why am I doing this? I need to work smarter. I need someone to help me make my calls. That was how I met Cathy, my loyal PA who stayed with me for 30 years.

In the beginning, she worked with me for just one day a week and she worked for four other people in the office for a day a week each too. The agreement was that I would pay her £10 an hour. She'd work four hours for me, so I gave her £40 at the end of every day. All the other people she worked with had the same arrangement. Except they didn't give her the £40. They would always come up with a reason why they couldn't pay her right then. They'd say she had not made any appointments, so they were not paying her. Or they would offer to cut her a deal where they would give her commission on the sale once they too got paid. Then they would come back from the appointment and say the prospect had not come through, even though they had. They were basically cheating her.

I was never like that and always paid up, on time, regardless of how successful she had been that day. I never queried it.

She could say, 'John, I made 50 calls, but I am afraid I have been unable to make you an appointment today.'

I would always say, 'Don't worry, Cathy, have another go tomorrow.'

The following day she would say to me, 'I have made you four appointments.'

I would always say, 'Well done, that is terrific!'

So our relationship developed because of that.

It is hardly surprising that, after a while, she began to work for me two days a week. Then two days turned into three days and eventually it became full time. She put all her trust in me because I was the only guy who always paid up. Trust and always playing with a straight bat is important in everything you do, whether it is dealing with clients or your team.

Everybody I have ever met has said I am so lucky that I found Cathy, because, as it turned out, she was a brilliant appointment maker. She is a real demon on the phone. But luck never came into it at all. Nearly all the other people she worked for let her down and I was the only one that didn't. This is why all my team have stayed with me for years, too. It is not sheer luck. It is because of the way I deal with them, thank them and make them know that I am so grateful for what they do for me. That is how it should be. Never be afraid to thank someone else, or compliment someone who has helped you get where you are. If you are nasty to people on the way up, I guarantee that when you start to come down there will be no one there to offer their support.

I always say that my staff are the best-paid people in Royston. If anyone on my team can get a better paid job elsewhere, I consider that to be a failure on my part. They all share in my goals and targets and if we hit them, you had better believe that they will be taken care of. I want them to be totally loyal, share in what I do and be part of it. They know that, if we are struggling for appointments or new business, they have an important job to do and they get on and do it. They do everything they can to help me get in more business. They use their own initiative.

Their work, and the bond of trust between us, is the foundation of everything I do. Together, we are a very powerful force to be reckoned with. That is what honesty and trust can do for you.

Step Seven: Set targets and keep records

There is no big secret to sales. No magic bullet that can make one person a better salesperson than the other. It is, purely and simply, a numbers game.

No matter how much difficulty you are in, you can always get out of it if you go and see enough people and make enough calls. I still remember sitting there with a phone book and an electoral register after Jim Wallinger had pushed me in the right direction when I was in a slump back in my Hambro Life days. I went through the register and noted down all the people in a road in a particular local area. I then cross-referenced my list to the phone directory, and if they were not listed in the phone directory I crossed them off the list. I then made call, after call, after call, night, after night, after night.

'Hello,' I said. 'You don't know me, but my name is John Cross and I am from Hambro Life Insurance. I wonder if you have a few moments to spare so I can talk to you about something?'

Some nights I made as many as 100 calls and sometimes 100 people said no, or please leave me alone, or worse. Then, one night, I made three appointments. The next day, I went to see three people and made three sales. I remember that feeling of euphoria after signing up those clients as clearly today as if it had happened yesterday. The next month, I made £1,600 commission on the back of all those calls, which was a lot of money in those days.

Of course, once I made a sale in one street, it was easier to make the next one. I could tell someone I had just seen their neighbour and that often opened doors, perhaps because they were curious to know what the other people in the street were doing.

The key is making the call. Ben Feldman, the American businessman who is widely thought of as one of the best salespeople ever, used to say that you must make the call even if someone is not going to answer, or will probably say no.

You will get lots of 'no' answers. But each time you get a 'no' is actually quite exciting because it is leading up to a 'yes'. As I said, it is a numbers game. You must always make the call, even if the man or woman at the other end is going to hurt you by not answering, or their secretary says they won't take the call. If you make enough calls things begin to happen. It is all about momentum. When you get a little *mo*, just keep going out there and making the calls, then you get a big *mo*. When you've got a big mo, you will get swept away. I guarantee it.

You should never be afraid to make a call, because there is always someone out there who will say 'yes, why don't you pop in and see me?' Most people don't make appointments to see someone for a business discussion unless they are interested in buying something. All a salesperson needs is the nerve to make the appointment in the first place. The one reason, more than any other, that people fail in this sales industry is through what is called 'call reluctance'. They are frightened to pick up the phone and dial in case they get a right uppercut. Well, you might and you might not. You'll never know unless you pick up that phone.

I've always found that it helps to have a definite reason to get out of bed in the morning and sell. People think I am mad, but every day I step outside my front door and think, who will buy today? There must be someone who will buy. I know if I make enough calls and see enough people there will be someone who will buy. That is absolutely 100% for sure. I might have to speak to five people, or 50, or 400 before someone does, but someone always will.

If you show me a salesperson who is not succeeding, I will show you a salesperson who is not seeing enough people. I'll know that for a fact and I won't even have to have met them. If you ask enough people you will get enough positive answers. If you want to be a success, you have to see enough people.

People often ask me what I would do if I ran out of prospects. This question always perplexes me. Surely this is a sign of a limited imagination? There are millions of people in the UK and billions more around the world. Once I have got through all of them, there is the universe after that!

I once had an office near the Gants Hill roundabout in northeast London. It is one of the busiest road junctions in the country and to me provided a perfect illustration of the numbers game. When salespeople came to me to complain that they were not able to get enough leads, I used to ask them to stand by the window and take a look out. To complete the effect, I'd leave the room and let them stand there for five minutes. When I returned I would ask, 'Did you see anything?'

'Yes,' they'd say, looking a touch mystified. 'I saw lots and lots of cars.'

'And yet you cannot find a single person to go out there to see,' I would reply.

There are always more people out there than you will ever get a chance to meet. So why not get out there and start seeing just how many might like to listen to your story?

Of course, if you are going to play the numbers game, you have to set yourself goals and targets. Back in my early days, my target was to make £35,000 a year. I wrote it down on a piece of paper and pinned it to the side of my bed. That meant that every night before I went to sleep I would see it and it was the same again first thing in the morning. I would wake up, see my note and be fired up by my ambitious goal. That helped me to believe that I would earn that money. I also knew that, in order to earn this money, I had to give a service, and in return for this service I would receive that coveted £35,000 of income. Every morning and every night I could touch it, feel it and smell it.

Today, my method is a bit more sophisticated and that piece of paper proclaiming that I wanted to earn £35,000 has grown to a comprehensive and detailed 40-page business document. This business plan contains very specific sales goals that are all based on solid fact, with reference to what I have achieved over the past four decades. I then extrapolate from that to see what I can achieve in the future and how much better I can be. I don't ever think, I'll try to match what I did last year, because that was pretty good. I think, how can I multiply my sales rate by a factor of five, six, seven or even ten? Then I visualise how I would feel if I managed that increase in sales. How excited would I be? How would my wife Sherry feel? How would the company react if I could achieve something like that, because it would be something no one had ever achieved before? Wouldn't that be something?

The plan is much more sophisticated than the paper I pinned up by the side of my bed, but the principle is the same. I look at this plan every day and carry it with me everywhere I go. It gives me just as much of a boost as that early scrap of paper, if not more.

Most salespeople don't plan to fail; they fail to plan. If you set a plan and work to it, day by day, hour by hour, week by week, year by year and keep chipping away it will happen, just as you imagined it.

You can never, ever lose sight of your objective. No one who ever stood on an Olympic podium with a gold medal around their neck achieved what they did because they lost sight of their original objective. Rest assured that every day when they woke up in the early hours, with hours of rigorous training ahead, their first thought would always be, I am going to win that gold.

Planning, prioritising and keeping a meticulous schedule is the key to sales success. If you can see on a daily basis how you are doing and where you are going next, it is easy to meet just about any income goal you choose. Even if things are looking tough, you will know that you can meet your targets just as long as you attend to the statistics.

If you are average you can always make a living, but if you are above average you can do really well. If you see five people a day and sell to one of them, you're doing OK. If you sell to two, or three, or four, you've really got it cracked.

Find your track

All salespeople need a track to run on. If you don't have a track to run on, how can you ever hope to win your 'race'? How can anyone ever know when they have reached their destination if they don't know where they are going?

The track I have chosen is represented in my BAFLAC report. BAFLAC is a readily available records system which stands for Business Analysis Folio for Life Assurance Consultants. It is a document which allows you to record every sale, both present and historic, matched against your own long and short-term goals. It was invented by my friend Paul Etheridge.

You don't have to keep a BAFLAC. You can find any method you like to create your own personal track. There are many other ways to record your progress, ranging from old-fashioned books to smart new computer programs. The point is: all salespeople have to have a track.

Every single Friday afternoon of my working life, for as long as I can remember, I have updated my BAFLAC. I cannot begin my weekend without doing it because I know I won't relax until it is done. This record tells me how many people I have seen that week, what I have earned over the past five days, my key sales ratios and how I am doing against my goal for the year. Once I have filled it in, I can tell at a glance whether I am up, or down, from the same time last year. It's all there in black and white. I keep it in my briefcase and I never go anywhere without it.

I never cease to be amazed that virtually none of my colleagues in sales keep a proper record. Indeed, most of them barely keep a record at all. I'd be prepared to stick my neck out here and predict that 99% of the people who read this book don't keep extensive records.

The reason why salespeople avoid meticulous record-keeping is perhaps quite simple. Records like my BAFLAC are a truth sheet. They force you to regularly look in the 'mirror' and admit that you didn't do what you said you were going to do, or perhaps were not quite as good as you thought you were. Many people don't like to admit they have failed or are struggling. It is a lot easier not to know.

The fact of the matter is: to be a success in sales, you must always keep records.

I also have a large Sasco planner on the wall of my office. All my appointments are recorded on there and my assistant puts a blue spot on a date every time an appointment is made. I know from my BAFLAC that I need to visit eight to ten appointments every week in order to reach my targets. Thanks to the Sasco and the blue dots I can always tell at a glance how I am doing.

I have always talked totally openly about my figures. What is there to be ashamed of? It is like nailing my colours to the mast and I have no problem with that. I am more than happy to face the truth about myself on Friday afternoon at four o'clock and then tell anyone who is interested how I am doing. I am totally at home with this silent pressure in my briefcase.

Indeed, many years ago, Prospect, a leading national life assurance magazine, asked me if I would be interested in writing a column based on my targets. I was asked to state my annual targets and then, in every issue of the monthly magazine, I had to record how I was getting on in meeting those targets. The by-line on the column was 'Mr X', which meant that I was not identified, but it did not take long for my colleagues in the industry to work out who it was. People kept coming up to me and exclaiming, 'You are Mr X, aren't you?' They probably guessed because I was one of the few people to keep such detailed records. I was perfectly happy to admit that I was the mysterious Mr X. But talk about nailing your colours to the mast! When your figures are being published every month in a national magazine there is no way you can possibly fail, is there?

Besides being highly motivational, there are other important reasons for keeping records too. Imagine for a moment that you are in a sales slump and you cannot understand why this might be. You feel like you are rushed off your feet, always chasing your tail to be everywhere at once and yet you just don't seem to be making any headway. If you had proper historical records, you would be able to look at them and see at once what was wrong.

Every time I am struggling, I just go back to my BAFLAC. I can see immediately that I must have, say, another 54 appointments between now and December, for instance, in order to hit my year's target. It will show me that, in order to make my target, I have to achieve an average of £X on every visit I make. It concentrates the mind because I know exactly how many people I am going to see and how much business I have to do.

If it is not going well, I can say to the people who make my appointments that we need to get at least another 20 this month to meet the goal. This will motivate them too because they will also get a bonus if we achieve what we set out to do when I wrote the plan.

If you don't have a track to run on and a firm idea of where you are going, you will always be vulnerable. Apart from not knowing how you are doing from one day to the next, you will have no firm direction. You'll chop and change your goals with the wind, which is always dangerous.

When I lay down my track at the beginning of the year, I always make sure to set my goals well ahead of what my company want me to sell. Therefore, by that definition, if I hit my personal target I will always be ahead of the company target.

Imagine, though, what would happen if you didn't have a record or a track to run on. What if your company suddenly came up with a new scheme which said that you needed to reach a target of £120,000 to become one of the elite salesmen that year? Most salesmen would say, 'OK, I'll try for that, then,' regardless of the fact that they had perhaps previously thought that they would aim for £90,000 that year. What happens then? Well, probably very little other than disappointment and failure. Why? Because they would be running on another track entirely. They're not on their old track any more, however tenuous it might have been. They'll be running in the outside lane of another person's track. If a runner switches tracks half way round, it should be no surprise to anyone if they don't get to the finishing line. No one who swapped tracks half way through a race would ever win a gold, silver or even bronze. You have to run on your own track.

Most companies accept that their sales force are pretty rubbish at setting targets and keeping records, so they do most of the work for them. They record their workers' figures and keep telling them how they are doing. This to me is a disaster. This means it is no longer the salesman's track; it is the company's track. The salesperson will have even less control over their destiny and will be vulnerable to any change made at the whim of their employer. Oh, by the way, their company could say, we've changed the annual target to £150,000 and put it on your sheet. If that happens, that salesperson is doomed. It must always be your goal, your target and your track.

Eliminate the prospects from the suspects…

As I have said before, everything I do is on an assumed basis; I assume the people whom I see will do business with me. Why else would they agree to having the meeting? I can do this because I always eliminate the prospects from the suspects: the wheat from the chaff.

Most salespeople spend far too much of their time chasing suspects, when what they should really be doing is only seeing prospects. The answer, which is glaringly simple when you think about it, is to find a way to eliminate the suspects from your list. If you can successfully differentiate between prospects and suspects, all you will be left with are prospects, not suspects. That is the aim of the game, no matter what you are selling.

It is a hard part of the job, but not impossible. As I have also already recounted, I always get clients to fill out a detailed questionnaire before our first meeting because it gives me all the information I need to properly prepare. It is a virtually foolproof way to eliminate suspects from prospects. Do you know why? Suspects are generally reluctant to give out any information. Prospects, on the other hand, fall over themselves to give me everything that I need in order to give them the very best advice.

If someone does not give me information, I don't chase. They are simply cast to one side. I am not interested in them. They are clearly not serious. Find me someone who will complete a five-page questionnaire and give me all the details that I need before I go and see them and I will show you someone who is very interested indeed in doing business with me. If somebody won't, they are just messing me around.

Many salespeople struggle with this concept because they are afraid that they will lose the prospect. They are afraid that they won't get the business. They can't seem to understand that they wouldn't have got the business anyway. I say, forget them. You would be better off using your time and energy on someone who was genuinely interested.

...and don't chase 'definite maybes'

I often play a game when I meet fellow salespeople.

I ask them, 'How are things going?'

'Oh, fine, fine,' they will probably reply with a feigned air of confidence.

I then press further and ask how much business they have done this year. By now, they will usually be getting a little unnerved and will say something abstract like, 'Oh, a fair bit.' But I will always push further and ask how much they have *really* done this year. If they haven't sloped off in disgust at this persistent questioning they might say, if I get this contract or that, I will be fine.

'Oh,' I say. 'So you are dead in the water, then.'

This will always cut them to the quick and they will look at me as though I have hurt them deeply. If they would only listen, I could tell them what their problem is exactly. There are chasing too many definite maybes. Definite maybes are the ones that you are chasing and chasing because if you get this one or that one it is going to make your year. Except definite maybes never happen.

Salespeople should never chase. They should create.

It is my firm belief that my colleagues in this industry waste too much time chasing and chasing definite maybes. I say, don't chase, chase, chase; create, create, create. Walk away from prospects if they don't bite. I guarantee that while you are spending the next three months chasing, people like me will be out creating something else and taking the bread from your table. Then, at the end of the year, when you don't get that big case you were relying on, the people who have created will be basking in the glow of all the business they have done while you were otherwise distracted.

All salespeople need to have things on the back burner: further business that is pretty certainly going to come in but as yet has no definite date. These are the people who have said yes, but have not yet paid their cheques or signed the paperwork. As I write this book, I probably have more than £1 million of applications on the back burner in my office in Royston. However, I barely give it a second thought. It would be a huge mistake to drop things from the front burner, i.e. pursuing new sales, because you are basking in the comfort of having plenty of things coming through 'at some point soon'.

Unfortunately, people become distracted by what they have on the back burner. They keep glancing over their shoulders at the back burner, instead of striding onwards and upwards to the next prospect.

I am always careful not to fall into this syndrome with my seminars. Yes, I always have a dozen or more booked in for the next 12 months and I know that means I will see hundreds of people who are keen to invest. Inevitably, I will get loads of leads to follow up from every event. However, that is no reason to take my foot off the accelerator and get complacent. A deal is never done until it is done. There are plenty of other things to do too.

Don't take your foot off the accelerator

It is a weakness in all salespeople that they take the foot off the accelerator once they hit their target. I regularly hit my year's target in September, but do you know what I do then? I then carry on working as hard as ever, right through to December, just to see how far I can beat my target by. My mantra has always been 'why would you settle for being average if you can be above average? Why would you settle for being ordinary if you could be extraordinary?'

I see so many people in this industry who could be really good, but then they turn out to be bone idle. They expect everything to come to them and just wait for it. They reach their target and grind to a halt. What they should be doing is getting out there and hustling every day, day after day, however well they have done in the months and weeks before.

There is nothing wrong with raising your target by 25% when you can see you are going to hit it well ahead of time. Indeed, it is always an admirable and potentially a highly lucrative thing to do. Most sales-led organisations have a bonus structure that is dictated by the amount of business that the individuals do. If you can see that you are within a crack of getting to the next level of bonuses, why wouldn't you want to try for it?

Going back to my days at McVitie and Price, if we reached our target we could choose prizes from a Littlewoods-style catalogue. This was great for me then, because Sherry and I had only recently got married, so we were able to furnish our new home with some of the electrical goods and domestic paraphernalia we needed. Over the years, the bonuses have become gradually more lavish. When I was at the office equipment firm, we were taken off to Paris if we achieved 25% over our target. Once I entered into the insurance business we were given the opportunity to attend conventions all over the world if we attained certain levels. As a consequence, I have travelled in style to many far-flung places. In recent years, the bonuses have turned into straight cash incentives.

The point is that companies are always good at providing carrots. You would be foolish not to take them, but you do have to play an active role in this and accept the motivation that your firm is offering you.

There are many ways of self-motivating, too. You will recall that I spoke about my wall chart earlier in this book. Every year it became adorned with pictures of my goals, from a gleaming Jensen Interceptor to Mickey Mouse beckoning me to Disneyland. It is all part of incentivising myself to go to the next level. Every year I come up with a different personal incentive to make sure I never stagnate and never drop off.

Maintaining the momentum is, of course, especially important when times are tough. However, no matter what I am selling, I will not let the economic situation dictate what my performance will be. I will always dictate what my performance will be. Everyone can get caught in the maelstrom of the winds of change, but they should still be able to hit their targets and beyond if they keep going out there and working their unique ability. It should be no different in a recession from at any other time. It just makes it more interesting. Confucius said it is good to be born in interesting times, and we have certainly been in interesting times in the last few years. The good salesperson just makes use of extensive targets and records to make sure they know what they are aiming for and then make it happen.

Step Eight: Never give in

A good salesperson never gives in. I don't mean they waste their lives yearning after the definite maybes when they should be looking for real doable opportunities. I mean that, when you set your sights on something and there is no real or logical obstacle to it happening, it is up to you to make it happen.

I learned this lesson very early on as a young salesman, dealing with a particularly hard-to-tie-down client in Loughborough. The firm that was in my sights was the holding company for a number of smaller businesses, so, as I was then selling office equipment, I was champing at the bit to add these various subsidiaries to my client list. I knew it would be a real coup and, of course, very lucrative in the long term. I picked up the phone and called and called and called in a bid to get an appointment with the fellow in charge of buying office equipment. Eventually, after I had been stonewalled a great many times, the buyer agreed to see me. I was cockahoop. This had the potential to be a huge account.

When the day of my appointment came I could barely contain the growing feeling of excitement in my belly. I carefully rehearsed my pitch on the two and a half hour journey up the M1 and anticipated any questions that might be asked.

When I walked into this company's grand office building I went straight to the receptionist and announced myself, explaining that I had an appointment with my contact. The lady took my details and duly rang through. Shortly after she had hung up the receiver, she turned back to me with a slight look of embarrassment on her face.

She said, 'I am afraid, Mr Cross, that your appointment is unable to see you today. He sends his apologies, but something has come up.'

I could hardly believe it. I was bitterly disappointed, but

immediately determined that I had to keep my cool. I explained, in my most professional manner, that I had just driven all the way from London. However, the by now slightly flustered receptionist just shook her head and apologised again. I got the impression that this was not the first time she had been left in such an awkward situation.

Finally I said, 'That is a shame. Never mind.'

I then strode across the reception area and sat down opposite her desk.

After a while, sensing that I was clearly not going anywhere, the receptionist began to look a little alarmed. Glancing around her, she left her post and came over to talk to me once again.

'Why are you waiting, Mr Cross?' she asked. 'I've told you he cannot see you. He is too busy.'

'Well,' I replied, 'I am here and I have driven all the way from London. I have no other appointments this afternoon, so I'll just wait and hopefully he might have some time later on.'

Well, as you can imagine, as the minutes ticked by, the receptionist felt more and more uncomfortable. She kept glancing in my direction and then quickly looking away. Eventually it must have got too much and she must have phoned through to her boss, because after an hour or so she suddenly announced, 'Mr Cross, he will see you now.'

I thanked the lady profusely and went on my way to the appointment I had worked so doggedly to keep. Then, before I strode into my meeting, I made sure that I had a warm smile on my face and was not showing a single trace of frustration at my long wait.

Do you know what happened next? My patience and determination were then rewarded with the account that I had coveted for so long.

Sometimes all salesmen and women have to be brave enough to stand up and be counted. That was what I did on that occasion and it was because I did so that I made the sale and won my sought-after account.

Now, some people may think me an obstinate fellow, but my reasoning behind staying put at this firm, even though I had been told my meeting was cancelled, was quite straightforward. This man had made the appointment and, therefore, the least he could do was see me to honour his side of the agreement. If he had seen me straight away and subsequently decided not to open an account with my firm, that would have been fine. It would have been disappointing, but that would have been his choice and his prerogative. However, I am not, and never have been, prepared to let anyone treat me as a nothing and a nobody. No one deserves to be treated like that and sometimes you just have to assert yourself to prove it.

I always assume when people make an appointment that they are going to see me. As a matter of course I write to confirm the appointment and I ensure that I always turn up on time. The least the other party can do is honour their side of the agreement. That is how it is and how it always should be.

It is not always easy to stand your ground. I do know that. Another of my most vivid memories from my early career involves a would-be client threatening me with a spanner! Even then, foolhardy or not, I didn't back off.

I had gone to the appointment at the prospect's workplace, which was a car repair garage in Luton. When I arrived, the person I had come to see was midway under a car and all I could see was the bottom half of a pair of greasy overalls and a large pair of steel toe-capped boots.

'Good morning,' I said, raising my voice to be heard above the clatter and whirring of all the machinery. 'It's John Cross, from Hambro Life, here for my appointment, as discussed over the phone.'

I was not for one moment prepared for what happened next.

The man pulled himself out from under the car, slowly stood up and then fixed me with a very malevolent stare. Then, his voice full of anger, he shouted, 'Well, you can eff off for a start!'

I did my best to remain calm and reminded him again that we had an appointment.

His voice now rose to a fever pitch and I took a step back as he yelled, 'I don't care if I made an effing appointment to effing see you. I don't want to effing see you now.'

Holding my ground, I told him that this was not very nice behaviour and he could at least talk to me like I was a reasonable person because I was, in fact, there at his behest.

Blow me down if the next thing that happened wasn't that he picked up a spanner and started to come towards me with the tool raised as though to hit me. All the while his face was utterly contorted in rage. I couldn't believe it, but decided to brace myself to appeal to his sense of reason one last time.

'I am sorry if I have upset you, but there is obviously a problem here,' I said, trying to keep my voice steady. 'Perhaps you could tell me what the problem is and I will see if I can help.'

Perhaps it was my refusal to be cowed by his threats, or perhaps his rage had run its natural course, but at that moment his whole attitude changed. He lowered the spanner and his shoulders slumped in resignation as he apologised and began to explain that he had just had a massive row with his wife.

'We have decided to get a divorce,' he said, the pain etched on his face. 'She wants it over with as soon as possible,' he added.

He went on to confess that he was almost blinded with anger, sorrow and fear at his hopeless situation and had barely known what he had been doing from the moment he had left home that morning.

Within ten minutes he was in tears and treating me like a long-lost friend. I can't even remember if I did any business with him that day, or even afterwards, but I did manage to calm him down. He realised it wasn't me that was a problem; it was him, and he was dumping his problems on me. He hadn't meant to and hadn't even realised that he was, until I had said, 'Hey, what is going on?'

The point of telling this story is not to show how brave I am (or perhaps foolish, not to walk away while I still can, depending on your point of view). It is merely to illustrate two very important points. Firstly that you should never, ever give in, even when the odds seem stacked against you. Secondly, we are all but a product of our experiences and we should use them all to make ourselves stronger.

What did I do after that man came at me wielding a spanner? Did I pack up and go home for the rest of the day to recover from my ordeal? Did I hell. I went straight out to find someone else to go and speak to, because that is what you have to do. A good salesperson can never surrender and never give in or be negative. If you do that you are dead in the water.

I always make it a rule that after every setback (and yes, I do get them too) I pick myself up, dust myself down and start looking for the next opportunity. I never give in. Every day I step out in the good faith that I will do a good job for my clients and all the people I will see that day. I truly believe that, too. If you never give in and go out every day believing you can do a better job than anyone else, you cannot help but succeed.

Convert a no into a yes

A friend of mine always used to borrow his neighbour's lawnmower every weekend to do his own lawn. He did this every week, year in and year out, until finally his neighbour had had enough. The next time the chap knocked on the door and asked to borrow it, the neighbour said, no, he couldn't borrow it.

'I can't have it?' asked my friend, a little taken aback.

'No,' said the neighbour.

'But I have borrowed it every weekend for the last 15 years,' said my friend.

'I know, but you can't have it this weekend,' replied the neighbour with a steady look.

'Do you mind if I ask you why?' enquired my friend.

'Because my mother-in-law is dead.'

My friend pondered the rather bizarre answer and perhaps foolishly decided to press his case. 'Your mother-in-law is dead? Well, I am very sorry to hear that, but do you mind if I ask you, what has that got to do with me not borrowing your lawnmower?'

'Nothing whatsoever,' replied the neighbour. 'But I figure that one excuse is as good as another.'

People will always find a reason why they don't want to do something. They may not articulate the real reason, but, if you want to sell something to someone who is not altogether sure, you had better listen out for what they are really trying to tell you.

Many salespeople take the old adage of 'never taking no for an answer' as carte blanche to badger and harangue wavering prospects until they say yes. This is completely the wrong approach, not least because the more you badger and harangue, the more likely the prospect is to retreat into their shell and resolve never to buy a thing from this pushy person. It can be completely self-defeating.

Nos can indeed be converted into yeses, but the process is far more subtle than trying to batter your prospect into submission. You have to understand why a prospect is saying no and the real reasons for their reticence. Then and only then can you work with them to find an accord that works.

In my experience, when a client says no, they don't really mean no; what they mean is 'I need some more information'. They need reassurance about the product and to understand that what they are doing is the right thing. There can be all sorts of reasons for this reticence and it is up to you, as an experienced salesperson, to find out what is behind their fears. Bashing them over the head is not the answer.

The reasons may not always make sense to you, but that is not the point. The point is, if the client has reservations of any sort, no matter how incomprehensible, you have to take heed.

Once, when I went to see a client, he told me very earnestly that he really wanted to do business with me, but sadly he couldn't.

'Why can't you?' I asked, very politely.

'Well,' he said, 'it is because of what they said in the House.'

'I am sorry, but I don't follow,' I said, continuing to be as patient as I could.

'About Prince Charles and Diana,' he replied, as though this should make sense to me, which of course it didn't.

'What about Prince Charles and Diana?' I pressed.

'Well, they are getting divorced. That's it. It'll mean the fall of the House of Windsor and there will be tanks on the street by the weekend.'

He really did believe that the royal divorce, which was admittedly quite high profile at the time, might actually make this happen. It was at this stage that I had to make my excuses and leave. I was experienced enough at that stage to know that sometimes you really can't change a client's mind and it would be far better to come back in a few months' time once he had seen that the predicted revolution had not, in fact, materialised. It, of course, didn't, and I did indeed return at a later date to do that piece of business. Occasionally it can take a little time to convert a no into a yes, but with a little patience and an open mind anything is possible.

A problem arising in recent years is that many prospects who are outwardly keen to do business will stall and say they can't do anything because of the uncertain economic situation. This really perplexes me and I always offer them the following scenario:

Imagine, I tell them, that I have just come into the room and said everything at Tesco is for sale at 20% off, but this only applies for one afternoon. Would you be tempted to go and buy anything? Or would you say, no, I will wait until tomorrow morning and pay full price?

Most people would say, don't be silly, of course we wouldn't wait to pay full price. We'd take full advantage of the sale.

Well, I tell them, the market is discounted by 20% or more at the moment, therefore there is a wonderful opportunity to get in at a 20% discount. By walking away because of the 'uncertain economic situation' you are effectively ignoring that opportunity.

If they don't do anything, I can virtually guarantee that when I see them in a few months' time the market will have gone up. Their hesitation will see them paying considerably more for their investment than they would have paid when we first had the discussion.

There are many other ways of looking at the reasoning behind a prospect's concerns, whatever they may be, and this is just one example. The important point is: if you take the time to listen to what prospects are worried about, it is always possible to make a perfectly logical argument which will appeal to all but the most under-confident ones.

I am never pushy, though. I never want to get into the battering-them-over-the-head scenario. I always emphasise to my clients that it is not my money; it is *their* money.

I tell them in all honesty, 'You are free to do with it as you wish, but if you want my advice as a financial advisor with many years' experience, I can tell you that now is the time to make the decision.'

The decision is, however, ultimately up to them. I honestly believe that and do everything in my power to make them believe that too.

That does not mean that I do not do everything I can to make the sale. But I do it by responding to the fears of my prospects and helping them to realise that they need to think about things in a different way from the way they thought in the first instance.

A successful salesperson learns how to appeal to their client's logic and get inside their brains. It is not as if you are trying to persuade them to do something against their better judgement. It is helping them do something they know they should be doing. What could be better than that?

Walk away with good grace – but still don't give up

If you can't persuade a prospect to do business with you, don't keep hammering away. As I have shown here, the haranguing approach is a waste of time for everyone. If someone says no, have the good grace to walk away. However, you should also stay very relaxed. After all, the time may not be right now, but things can and do always change.

Whenever I can see that a client is really not ready, or willing, to make a commitment, I always reassure them that they don't have to do anything immediately. But I do give it one last try. In my line of work, I remind them that they came to my seminar, filled in my form and said that they wanted to change, say, their inheritance tax position, for example. Without being at all pushy, I finish up by saying, 'If you don't do this now, how are you going to improve your inheritance tax position?'

Then I just shut up and wait.

If the shutters come back up completely and the prospect is still resolutely not buying, I say, fine. I ask their permission to put them on my 'definite maybe' list, which always raises a smile, and finish by saying that if and when they feel I can help they should by all means give me a call. I am always ready and willing to be of service.

The difference between me and most salespeople is that after experiencing a rejection like this, when I walk out the door, get in my car and drive off, I have not forgotten the prospect who turned me down. I do not mentally write them off as a time waster or a fool. I am never bitter or cross at being thwarted. The one-time prospect will indeed go onto my mailing list and from that time on they will receive regular contact and further invitations to my seminars whenever there is one being held in their area.

I find all sorts of ways to maintain a connection with people who have said no, because, who knows, they may well bear fruit in the future. I send them regular copies of my own quarterly Investor magazine, which contains useful articles and advice. Plus, twice a year, I send out a bespoke CD on which fund managers are recorded giving priceless details of what they are doing with their portfolios and giving their expert views of what is happening in the market.

I know that all of this makes me completely different from all the rest of the salespeople this potential client has ever seen. They may have said no, but, when they receive all this information and regular updates on the market, they can't help but see that they don't get this sort of attention from their high street bank or other financial advisors. NatWest, or Barclays, or HSBC don't keep in constant touch with such useful information. The banks don't offer to send out their most experienced advisors at the client's convenience. These institutions don't give away expert knowledge from top advisors for free.

Gradually it dawns on them that maybe they were wrong to say no.

They do, of course, always have the option to say, 'Go away and leave me alone.' That is their prerogative. I enclose a form to this effect in all my mailings and will honour it immediately by removing them from the list. All they have to do is say the word.

The important thing is to give prospects a regular opportunity to reconsider that no and make it a yes.

It may take years, it may only be months, but I guarantee that in many, many cases that person who said no will call me back in. They always say the same thing when they do, too. They tell me that they are annoyed that they didn't do what I told them when we first talked and now they would like to go ahead

My philosophy is that every time someone says no to you, you are but one step away from a yes. Keep in touch, keep the faith and people will come back. They do.

If you don't try to grind your prospects down by badgering and haranguing, but instead just keep in touch with regular, helpful updates, you will win their respect. Once you have got their respect it does not matter whether they buy from you at that moment in time or not, because they will in all probability buy from you later.

If one client says no, always keep in touch, but in the meantime move on and find another, more willing one. If one door closes, there are plenty more which will open, but you will never find them if you are hanging around that closed door.

I am not just waiting for the call. I see many, many other people in the meantime. All I have done is eliminated the suspects from the prospects, but that doesn't mean they can't become prospects again. So just keep in touch, keep in touch and keep in touch. Keep the hopper full. One day either the prospect will say, 'Leave me alone,' or they will say, 'I am ready to see you now to do some business.'

I always act in exactly the same way as this if I ever lose a client. It is a rare occurrence because all my clients get Rolls-Royce service, but, if I do, I tell them that I am very sorry to see them cash in their investments and urge them to keep in touch. Then, once again, I keep in touch by inviting them to future seminars and sending them the magazines and CDs. I never respond to clients who cash in their investments by declaring, or even implying, that they are daft for changing. That would be insulting their intelligence. I just remind them that I will always be there and stay in touch. Then I do just that.

Think on your feet

In my spare time, for my own relaxation and enjoyment, I was a referee for over 30 years and until quite recently I used to referee football matches every weekend. The experience taught me many useful lessons, which I have often applied to my sales jobs. Perhaps the most important lesson of all that I took away from my hobby is the importance of thinking on your feet. This quality, perhaps above all others, can help turn a hopeless situation into a good one.

I'll give you an example. As a fully qualified soccer referee, I was once invited to referee a game between English and German schoolboys that was being played over in Germany. It was a hard-fought match, but with ten minutes to go the game was still a stalemate at one-all. With tensions rising, suddenly the English centre forward broke away and went charging down the middle of the pitch. However, as he got to the edge of the penalty area, a German defender chopped him down. It was a clear penalty. Except the German boys went mad, absolutely mad and refused to accept the ruling. I couldn't understand it. Thinking I had perhaps missed something, I went over to consult the linesman, who had already given the penalty signal symbolised by a flag on the chest.

'John, it is a clear penalty,' he said, with a shrug.

'I thought so too,' I said.

I gave a penalty. The English centre forward booted it into the back of the net and the match was then at two-one.

Then, in the last minute, something extraordinary happened. The English boys broke away down the wing, the winger kicked the ball over and the English centre forward did a classic header, bang, into the back of the net. It was a truly wonderful goal. The only problem was it was offside.

As I was lifting my whistle to blow for offside, I looked around me. The linesman had given the goal, the English boys were celebrating and the Germans all had their heads bowed in defeat. In fact, the only person who didn't think it was a goal was me. So I thought about it. In my view, a final score of three-one without a disputed penalty was a much better outcome than two-one with a disputed penalty, so I gave the goal. Nobody queried it. The only person who ever thought it was not a goal was me.

In my view, it is a vital skill for a salesperson to be practical and learn how to deal with all the things that come their way. You have to be prepared to play things by ear, go with the flow and make fast decisions. Obviously, in the case of the schoolboys' football match, my decision was not to make a decision, but the important take-home message was that fast thinking rescued a potentially awkward situation.

I am fortunate that I have always been able to think very quickly on my feet and this has helped me a great deal in my choice of career. As I have shown in this chapter, a client's objections may not always be rational, or even understandable, but a canny salesperson has to learn to deal with them just the same. Think fast and you will be able to turn any situation to your favour.

Your next triumph is always around the corner

People reading this chapter may say, ah, it is all very well for you, but it is not always easy to keep slogging away and never give in when you get one knock-back after the other.

Well, sometimes it will be tough, particularly in the early days. However, there is one thing you must always remember.

Your next triumph is always around the corner.

It is true. Even when things look at their bleakest, it only means that you are another step closer to turning things around. You just need to keep the faith and keep working hard.

I once worked with a nice young lad called Vic Ketch. Unfortunately, his wife made it very clear that she didn't approve of his choice of career and was particularly unhappy about him going out to see female clients. She was very jealous and suspicious, although Vic never ever gave her reason to be.

Eventually, the pressure from home got too much and Vic reluctantly agreed to give up his sales career and try his luck elsewhere. He came in to my office to see me just before he quit the firm. His shoulders were slumped and he seemed thoroughly dejected, yet resigned to moving on.

I had always got on well with Vic, so he asked me if I would like to take on his client list. He had a number of prospects whom he had been to see and was hoping to close, but now he was unable to see it through. I told him that I would be honoured to do so and reassured him that if any prospects did sign on the dotted line, I would make sure that he got the commission due to him. Soon after that Vic left and I, for one, was very sorry to see him go.

The next day, I set about tackling his list. The very first one I called was a pension case. I explained to the chap on the other end of the phone that I had worked with Vic Ketch, who had sadly left the firm, but I would be happy to do all that I could to help him with his case. The man said that was a real shame because Vic was a lovely guy, but he would like to see me nevertheless. As soon as I got in to see this prospect he told me that he had decided, on the basis of Vic's earlier proposal, to put the entire pension business of his not insubstantial company with my firm. I got all that pension business because Vic never got the chance to go back and see his prospect, even though he had put in all the hard work. It was my first big pension case and I must confess I did think, goodness, I didn't do anything to get this except be nice to Vic. When I told Vic about it later, even he was surprised that I had been able to just walk in on the Monday morning and make a sale.

In actual fact, though, I didn't really make the sale at all. Vic did. His prospect made the decision and I just took the order.

The point of this story is: Vic gave up just before making his greatest ever achievement. Vic is not alone. It always amazes me that many, many salespeople throw in the towel when their greatest triumph is just around the corner. If you want to succeed, you must always keep on keeping on and always believe that you are going to go out there and make a sale. Because if you do, you will.

Step Nine: Work like bloody hell

When my dad was a 15-year-old lad he went to the nearby market in Leicester. There, among the noise and bustle of the street vendors selling their wares, he spotted a man who was selling what appeared to be single white envelopes. It piqued my father's curiosity because this fellow had attracted quite a crowd. People were standing entranced three deep around this vendor's stall and he was entertaining the assembled throng with a quick-fire, jokey patter. As my father drew closer, he heard the man explain that each of these envelopes contained a guaranteed way to make a fortune.

'Yes, folks, for just 6p you too can learn the secret to a comfortable and happy life with all the money you could ever need!' shouted the market trader, holding the envelopes aloft, fanned out like a pack of playing cards. 'Go on! Who wants to make their fortune?'

My father thought about it hard because 6p seemed a lot of money to pay, but his curiosity got the better of him and he could not resist seeing what was inside this mystery envelope. He stepped gingerly up to the stall, clutching his coins, and told the trader that he would like to buy one of the envelopes.

'Good lad,' said the man, handing him one of the precious envelopes with a conspiratorial wink. 'Now, off you go, walk around the corner to open your envelope. But remember: don't let anyone see what is inside, because it is only meant for you. Good luck!'

My father took the envelope and walked off with his prize, now thoroughly curious about what it might contain.

As he rounded the corner with his heart beating loudly in his chest with excitement, he examined his purchase carefully, almost afraid to open it. The front of the envelope had the words 'guaranteed to make your fortune' in large print on the outside.

As he slid his finger inside the seal to rip it open, my dad began to imagine all sorts of things that might lie within.

Once it was open, it revealed a small, folded piece of paper. Opening it out, my father began to read the text.

It said, 'Work Like Bloody Hell, from first thing in the morning until last thing at night, seven days a week.

'That is the way to make your fortune!'

This brief, yet powerful, missive obviously had a huge impact on my dad, because 30 years later he told me all about it and it has stuck with me all my life too.

It is true. If you want to get anywhere in life, you have to work like bloody hell. It doesn't matter if you are an entrepreneur, an accountant or running your own market stall. If you work hard, you will succeed.

Most salespeople don't work like bloody hell. In fact, in my experience, they are bone-idle beggars. Indeed, I often think that is why people choose sales as a career. They think that it is a great way to make a few bob without too much effort. They don't understand that to be successful, you have to work pretty hard, especially in your early days.

A job in sales is not the 'easy option'. Yes, you can make a very good living out of sales as a career, but you have to work at it. And keep on working at it.

...But work smart

On a company convention some years ago, a man came up to me to ask my advice. He was producing around £100,000 a year in commission and his target was to double this to £200,000.

'You are successful, John,' he said. 'How can I get from £100,000 to £200,000? I am working my socks off, but don't seem to be doing any better whatever I try.'

I had a chat with him to find out a little more. He seemed to be doing all the right things, but was still clearly struggling and was obviously very frustrated by his lot. Then, in passing, I mentioned that I would get some information that might help over to his PA. Suddenly, out of nowhere, he exploded in rage.

'I haven't got one of them,' he yelled, almost purple with fury. 'Why the hell would you need a PA? Why give someone money when you can just as easily do it yourself? That is ridiculous!'

I waited until he had calmed down a little and said, 'If you are serious about doubling your turnover, you can't do it on your own. It is just not possible.'

Then, of course, it all came out. This poor chap was already working 18 hours a day, six and a half days a week, yet he was proud of the fact he did not pay a penny to anybody. He was working entirely alone with no back-up support or administrative staff whatsoever. Try though I might to persuade him otherwise, though, he resolutely ignored all my entreaties to get some help and employ people to make his appointments for him. He just couldn't see the point. Eventually he sloped off in a rage, furious that I just 'didn't get it'. I dread to think where he ended up.

This chap's mistake was that he had taken the 'work like bloody hell' formula in the wrong way. He thought the only way to get to the top was to toil for as many hours as possible. Sadly, though, he is not alone.

Most people confuse working hard with working long hours seven days a week and never taking a break. You don't have to do that. You just have to work smart.

Early on in my career, when I too believed that I had to work all hours in order to do well, my strategic coach Dan Sullivan gave me some very good advice.

'Only do the things that you are good at and are actually paid for,' he said. 'You should never be doing anything else. You will be wasting your time.'

I thought about what he had said and realised that he was right. Before he said this to me, I was only spending about 70% of my time actually selling. The rest of my time was consumed by making appointments, setting up seminars and doing all the other admin stuff I thought needed to be done. I hadn't really thought that there was any other way of working. On reflection, though, I realised that I was wasting a great deal of my time and not really using my real strengths – i.e. selling – to the full.

To wean me off this, Dan advised that I take 50% of that 30% where I did things other than selling and delegate those tasks to someone else. So I did. The following year, I took 70% of the time that was still being devoted to tasks elsewhere and delegated that too. On the third year, I handed all the rest of the periphery over.

Since then, I haven't made my appointments. I don't organise my seminars. I don't handle any account details. In fact, I don't do any backroom stuff at all and don't even drive myself to appointments. I leave that to my PA, my sales assistants and my chauffeur, all of whom are more than capable of doing those tasks. Indeed, they are far more capable than me. I just sit down with them, agree what needs doing and when, and then let them get on with it. All I do is sell, sell, sell, which is what I am best at and enjoy. It works. Perfectly.

If you are a salesperson, you should be concentrating on sales. Why would you do anything else? After all, how is it you earn your money?

The best way to work smarter (and therefore harder) is to get someone else to do what you don't have to do. Look at it this way: if your assistant's time is worth a £10 an hour but they free you to go out and work full pelt and earn £100 an hour then you will still be £90 an hour better off.

For me, giving away the parts of the job which were not an effective use of my time was an easy thing to do once I woke up to what a fool I was being. However, I do know that many people find this very difficult. Indeed, some people find it altogether impossible. They won't let go because they think no one can do any single part of the job as well as they can, besides which if they do it all themselves they can keep all the money to themselves. But, as you can see here, the maths just doesn't add up.

I assume that people get sucked into working for hours and hours because they believe that is what they have to do in order to be successful. Yet, aside from the fact that it makes sense to delegate parts of the job you don't need to be doing, I strongly believe that the longer you work, the less efficient you become. Long hours are actually totally counterproductive. The fact is that, most of the time, if people stopped working after about six or seven hours, it would probably be spot on and they would achieve all they needed to achieve. Anything after that is just wasting their time, because if anyone slogs away at full pelt for any longer I guarantee you that they will be too tired to work efficiently.

The other mistake that is commonly made in this respect happens when people do eventually get someone who can take on parts of their job. They can never resist constantly looking over their assistant's shoulder to check they've done it properly. Apart from the fact that this is a complete waste of time (you got them in to free your time so you could sell, not look over their shoulders), in my view, one of the worst things anyone can do is ask someone to do something and then check if they have done it. That just undermines their confidence. I always work on the assumption that if I ask someone to do something, then it gets done. And it does.

Most importantly, though, it is just logical to bring in other people and work as a team to build up a business. The alternative is to end up flogging yourself to death for a lot less money. What is the point in that?

Too many people wait too long. They don't bring people in and get the help they need until they are drowning. Then they say, 'I am drowning, get me some help!' What they should have done is got some help before they even got into the water.

If you have people to help you, you won't drown. You stay above the water line.

I have never looked back since I decided to take on people to do some of my work for me while I stuck to what I was good at. These days I don't average more than a 35-hour week and this year I will only be working 30 weeks out of the 52. But, back when I started out, it did not embarrass me to work 80 to 100 hours a week if I had to. I had my goals and my targets, and worked until I achieved them. I knew that I had to put the time in, in order to achieve those goals and be a success. And I did. But I always took on help where I needed it.

Steal if you have to!

Ah, you may say. It is all very well for you, John. You are a wealthy man. You can afford to take on extra help. Me, I am juggling a family, a large mortgage and other punishing financial commitments and I can't afford to employ any staff.

Do you know what I say to that? Steal the money you need to take on new staff if you have to! Actually, I don't mean that, but it is about an attitude of mind. If you want something enough, you must be prepared to do virtually anything to get it.

In the early days, when I first decided that I wanted to do seminars, I didn't have any money. Not a spare penny. Indeed, I owed quite a lot on my own mortgage and was finding the payments quite tough. However, after working out the cost of the seminars, I knew that I needed at least £4,000 to put on my first one. That is a lot of money today and an awful lot of cash 30 years ago.

After scratching my head for a little while, trying to think of a way to raise the money, I found out that American Express were offering a £4,000 allowance if you took out one of their credit cards. So that was what I did. I got an American Express gold card and used it to fund my first seminar. I worked on the assumption that if I could make the seminar a success, I would be able to pay the money back from all the commission that I would earn.

Actually, I got it wrong. Very wrong. As it turned out, I had to do three seminars before I started to make any money. What I had not allowed for was the fact that there is a learning cycle to seminars and the payback was not instantaneous. The concept of seminars was something new for me and I did not know the best way to follow up on the leads afterwards, not least because the events brought in a new type of customer. It took time to learn how to deal with the new clients and give them what they wanted.

Fortunately, I realised this quite quickly and, undeterred, set about raising some extra funds. I spent some days putting together an extensive business proposal and went to the bank to ask for a £10,000 overdraft. To my surprise, they said OK. Yes, I was then £14,000 in debt, but I had secured enough money to run two more seminars. Talk about putting your money where your mouth is! But, when all is said and done, there is no better way to motivate yourself every day than to be in significant debt.

There is always a way if you want something enough. Always a way. My perseverance and investment in my future was rewarded. After about a year, I began to get my investment back through commissions, just as I had expected, albeit slower than I had first calculated. After that, though, I got better and better at my events and managed to pay back all my debts quite quickly.

Sometimes it takes a leap of faith, but if you want to be a success you have to do what it takes. I always remember speaking to an American salesman, Calvin J Hunt. He explained he had taken on a large office and loads of staff to go with it.

People said to him, 'Calvin, you've got too many people for what you are doing.'

'Yes, you are right,' he would reply. 'But there won't be nearly enough people for what I am doing next year.'

This is an interesting approach. What he was saying, and I totally agree with him, is that you have to be prepared for the next stage. That does mean that sometimes you will need to stretch yourself, but, as long as you go into it with both eyes fully open, success should be right around the corner.

Manage your time efficiently

These days, as I have already said here, I only work a 35-hour week for 30 weeks a year. There are two key reasons that I am able to do this successfully. Firstly, I have a hugely efficient back-office operation which manages a great deal of my workload. Secondly, I have carefully honed my time management skills so not a moment of those 35 hours is wasted.

I dictate all my reports to my clients in the back of the car, directly after my meetings with them. That way the information is still fresh in my mind. The tape then goes directly to my secretary, who will then be asked to insert a number of standard paragraphs into that report, which again cuts down on the amount of time I need to spend on each one. I am similarly happy to sit in my car through lunchtime to deal with as much paperwork as I can. I have never seen the point of spending the time in the office, gossiping with colleagues. Indeed, I spend so little time in the office that when I am there people always want to talk to me about business-related issues and not waste time on idle chat about whether I saw some football match or other last week. It just doesn't come into the conversation.

I have a natural ability to avoid dealing with time wasters among potential clients, too, because there will always be some. I will very quickly sum up if I am with a time waster and, if I am, I am out of there in ten minutes flat. Why would anyone want to spend time with people who are total, utter time wasters? I don't.

If you learn to utilise your time effectively, you won't ever have to go for the 'work like bloody hell' option of working 48 hours a week.

There is, however, a very important proviso to all of this. I never, ever scrimp on the time that I spend with clients. I will always, always go to see someone, even if they don't have anything to invest then and there. That is what makes me different.

Many a time I have been contacted by clients who say they'd like to see me but don't want to 'drag me all the way to' wherever. I always reply, 'Of course I don't mind; you are a client.' I mean it, too. If they want to invest more money, that is fine, but if they wanted to see me anyway, I would still go to see them. That is what my job is all about. It is about under-promising and over-delivering. I am genuinely happy to go and see clients, whatever the reason, and most importantly they know that too.

Get a round tuit

Every person who ever comes to one of my seminars is always given a circular coaster in the pack that they take away at the end of the session. Printed on the coaster is the simple phrase 'A Round Tuit'. It is a humorous reminder that we all need to get around to doing what we know we should do. In their case, it means 'get on with sorting out your finances'. Now that they have their very own round tuit, they cannot say that they will get around to it some day, because they already have one!

The same thinking could, however, be applied to most salesmen. They never seem to be able to get around to doing the things that will make a real difference to their lives. They ignore things that would make things easier for them and mean that their efforts would be used most effectively.

I'll give you an example. Most service-based companies have what I call orphans. These are the former clients of a salesperson who has left the company and gone elsewhere. At any one time there can be literally hundreds of these in any one organisation. The idea is that when this happens, the company divides up the orphans and allocates them to the existing team to look after.

What do you think happens then? Zilch. The person who acquires these orphans does nothing. Not a phone call, not a letter, nothing. Many times I have asked colleagues, why have you not contacted this list of orphans that you have been given? The reply is always the same.

'I just have not got around to it,' they say.

'Why not?' I ask.

'Because I am busy looking for new business,' they reply in all seriousness, not for one moment realising the irony of the statement.

They don't seem to understand that, with the minimum of effort, these orphans may easily give them pots of new business. They are, after all, already pre-disposed to working with the company and have been happy to give us their investments before.

When I joined my present company, I asked them for a list of all the orphan clients we had in the company. I had to do a lot of badgering to get the names, but eventually they gave them to me. However, as I couldn't cover the whole of the UK, they gave some to salesmen in Manchester, some to salesmen in Leeds and some to salesmen in Bristol.

The moment I got the list of orphans, I immediately wrote to every single one of them. I said, 'As you know you are with my company. You did business with the company X years ago and recently no one has been looking after you or servicing your business. I would like to meet with you and take on that responsibility.'

I did so much business from those leads that after the first two years I stopped counting. Believe it or not, I still deal with many of those original orphans even today.

What do you think happened to the orphans who lived in and around Manchester, Leeds and Bristol? Nothing. After a couple of years, when I told the company what I had done with my orphans, they said, do you know what, John, most of the other salesmen didn't do a damn thing with them. Can you believe it?

To me, ignoring such an obvious opportunity is inconceivable. Whenever I get a new orphan client, the first thing I do is call them up and say hello. I introduce myself as their new contact and say I'm very happy to come and see them at their earliest convenience. Failing that, is it OK to put you on our mailing list? I'll say. I take the time to sound them out to see how they'd like to deal with me. One year I did a £350,000 investment for an orphan client. The moment I called him he told me he was so glad that I had taken over and was looking after him so well. He really appreciated it. That is what it is about. It is about looking after people. If you look after people and let them know you do care, it just falls into your lap. It is not even hard work. It is just making sure you get around to it.

Many salespeople are simply too disorganised. Others are just plain lazy. But, either way, it all adds up to the same thing. They run around saying they are looking for new clients, but just don't seem to get the essential things done even though those things are completely straightforward and would clearly be to their full advantage.

Ignoring the orphans is not the only example of this negligent behaviour.

One year a colleague came to me and said he would like to give seminars a go.

'Would you help me, please?' he asked.

I invited him to come along to one of my events to see what I did and then offered him a lot of help and advice to set up his own. He duly organised his own seminar and, after the event, I dropped by his office to see how he had done.

'Excellent, thank you, John,' he said, waving his hand across a stack of papers on his desk. 'I have more than 100 leads.'

'That is brilliant,' I said, genuinely pleased for him. 'Let me know how you get on.'

A month later I went into his office and there, on the corner of his desk, was the pile of leads. They appeared to have been completely untouched.

'What happened with those leads?' I asked.

'Yes, I must get around to following those up,' he replied absent-mindedly.

'Why haven't you done anything yet?' I asked, genuinely perplexed and not a little exasperated.

'Well, I went on holiday for two weeks a week after the seminar and things have just piled up a bit since then,' he said.

This of course raised a number of questions, not least of which was: why did he book the seminar for when he did, if he knew he had a holiday just around the corner? And why did he not get on to those leads straight away as soon as he got back?

You will probably not be surprised to hear that when I passed by his office four weeks later, the leads were still sitting on the corner of his desk, by now covered in a fine layer of dust. By then, of course, all those people who had expressed a real interest in doing some business were long gone. All I could think was, what a waste of everyone's time that was.

The same goes for referrals from existing clients. I always follow up when my clients tell me that so and so might be interested in doing some business with me. In my view, you can't go far wrong by dealing with these people, not least because your existing client will already have done half the selling job for you. If you get a recommendation from a client, it is worth 1,000 telephone calls. Why would you ignore that?

Yet, while we all get these referrals, so many of my fellow salespeople don't ever seem to get around to following them up, because they are 'too busy' with other things. They are just not working smart.

Working like bloody hell is the way to make your fortune, just as my father's envelope predicted. However, it doesn't have to be punishing if you get help, work smart and don't ignore the obvious opportunities. Sometimes things are virtually handed to you on a plate. Any salesperson would be a fool not to pick them up and run with them.

Step Ten: Have fun

It has changed today, but, many years ago, the Oxford Dictionary definition of a salesman was along the lines of 'someone who sells a person something they don't want'. That always made me laugh because, to me, that is so untrue. Apart from the fact that it is almost impossible to sell something to someone who doesn't want it, it is also completely wrong.

These words were brought back to me in a very amusing way when I was on holiday in Turkey and visiting a local bazaar in Istanbul. There I was with Sherry, wandering around row upon row of literally hundreds of busy stalls. The cacophony of noise, colours and smells was totally overpowering to every one of our senses. Everywhere we walked, vendors were yelling out, trying to get us to step into their shops and give them our precious business. Then, all of a sudden, a man stepped out in front of us. He flashed us the most charming of smiles and threw his arms wide open, saying, 'Come on in and buy something you don't want!'

I could not help laughing. Nor could Sherry. It was one of the funniest sales lines I had ever heard. It kept a smile on my face for the rest of the day and still makes me chuckle now whenever I think about it.

Selling should be fun. Yes, you have to work hard and a lot of people will say no. Some of them may even be rude to your face and make unkind comments. But the lesson I have learned is: if you don't keep a sense of humour and a light heart, you will never survive a career in sales. You will just get ground down by the rejections and lost prospects. If you carry on letting it get to you, you will never make it. There is no way you can succeed.

I always do my damnedest to make my clients smile because I know if I can do that it means they are relaxed. If a client is relaxed, half the battle is won. Just as importantly, though, it means I am enjoying myself too. One of the great things about life is if you enjoy doing what it is you do, whatever you do is effortless.

What can be more important than doing a job you love? We devote so many hours of our lives to our jobs, it is essential that we derive satisfaction and joy from them. If you don't feel that way about your day job you should try your hand at something else.

Anyone who has ever done any selling will always readily recount their experience of their first ever sale. They will remember as if it were yesterday. The thrill of the moment when anticipation and anxiety suddenly transform into a feeling of excitement and elation will be etched on their brain. You have made that sale! It is a time when you know, you just know, that this is the best ever job in the world and the rewards are far more than the pound or dollar it puts in your pocket.

Do you know what? After 50 years of pounding up and down the nation's highways and byways, I still feel the same way every time I close a sale. I have never, ever lost that heady feeling that I got from my first ever sale and can honestly say I have got it every time I have made a sale since. I have never lost the enthusiasm, that feeling of magic and that desire to get out there and do it all again. I don't care if it is a £10,000 ISA or a million-pound bond. I am just as thrilled to hear those magic words, 'Where do I sign?'

A great deal of why I still feel that buzz is down to the fact that I don't let my job become boring, or repetitive, or routine. I consciously take pleasure in every aspect of my job, particularly in the long-term relationship I have with all my clients.

It is an honour and a privilege to spend time with a fellow human being. I know I can sit with a client for an hour and hear them saying something to me that I might remember for the rest of my life. Or I might say something to them that they will remember for the rest of their lives. What a rewarding experience it is to be able to do that. It is truly a privilege to be in a position from which you can influence people and help them see what they should be doing with their hard-earned money. By doing what I do I am simply helping them along the way. What could be more fulfilling than that? I am not selling anyone something they don't want.

An important part of this relationship is always treating people with respect and courtesy. My longest-standing clients, who have been with me for over 30 years, are always addressed by their formal titles of Mr and Mrs Smith. I would not dream of calling them by their Christian names, despite the strong bond we have built up over the years, and I believe that they really appreciate the respect that I continue to show them. But that doesn't mean that I don't have fun with Mr and Mrs Smith, or indeed any of my other clients. Being respectful does not mean that you can't have a great relationship with people, or a jolly good laugh. You can and I do.

For me, much of the joy of a long-term relationship with my clients shines through because I am happy to see them every time I visit. They are happy to see me, too. They smile when they greet me and my smile back is genuine.

I always try to keep the mood light in my meetings, despite the sometimes dry subjects I am there to discuss. One of my favourite games is when a would-be client asks me anxiously if I have a minimum investment amount. In other words, would I refuse to deal with them if they were only able to invest a very small quantity of cash?

I always reply, 'Yes, I do, actually,'

'Oh,' they reply, usually shifting uncomfortably in their chair. 'What is the minimum amount?'

'How much do *you* have to invest?' I ask in return.

'£10,000,' they'll say, or '£5,000' or even '£3,000'.

Quick as a flash, I will come back: 'Isn't that amazing? That is my exact minimum amount!'

I always do it with a warm smile and they can immediately see that I am joking. But, in truth, I never do look at a sale on the basis of the size of the cheque. What is important is that I have now got this person as a client and they trust and like me. That is half the battle won. After that, who knows what they will invest in the future? As I showed earlier in this book, little acorns can, and often do, grow into towering oaks.

Sometimes, humour is a great asset when I want to help a client to reassess their priorities. For example, I have a lovely client with whom I have worked for many years. He is a very well-to-do company director with assets well in excess of £12 million. Yet he flies all over the world in the economy seats of the cheapest budget airline he can find. That would be all well and good if he were flying short-haul for a weekend break, but, best intentions aside, anyone who flies half way across the world in this way is hardly likely to get to their destination in good shape to do business. I could see that it was starting to become a real problem for him, not least because he was not getting any younger. In the end, I had to use a bit of gentle teasing to loosen him up a little and tell him he was being foolish in the nicest possible way.

Finally I said, 'For goodness' sake, by the time you get to America your shares will have gone up or down by a damn sight more that the cost of a first-class airfare. You won't even notice the difference!'

He got the point and visibly relaxed. The next time we met he described in vivid detail the luxurious first-class flight he had enjoyed to Japan for a corporate meeting.

Humour and levity can come from many sources, but they make a huge difference. Get the tone right and you will really stand out from the crowd.

In the early days of my career, I always used to wear a bowler hat to every meeting I attended, long after they were no longer commonplace. My clients loved it and it never failed to raise a smile. It helped to open doors, too. I still remember now going to see one company, where the receptionist assured me the person I wanted to see never entertained salespeople under any circumstances. I was lucky enough that the very person I was trying to see happened to walk by reception while I was trying to convince the receptionist to buzz me through.

'Ah,' he said, spotting the smart bowler hat, 'you are one of the old school. I like that.'

He sat down with me then and there, much to the receptionist's chagrin. He confirmed that he did not normally see commercial travellers, but said he liked my style and was intrigued by my smart dress. From the moment we met, we immediately had a relaxed rapport. Guess what? I made my sale that day and it turned out to the biggest order I had ever had at that time. That is all you need: a smile, a cheery disposition and maybe a bowler hat too.

There has never been a moment when I have not enjoyed doing what I do as a salesman. Ever. I have always loved every minute. I knew I wanted to do it long before I left school, and here I am at 68 years of age and I still want to do it. My feelings have not changed one iota and my family know well not to ever mention the dreaded 'R' word: retirement!

I always see the funny side of things, even if it is not immediately apparent. If you find a way to look on the positive side, you will never get laid low by the negative side.

Give people a memory

A colleague once came in to see me and said that he was really struggling with what to get his wife for her birthday.

'John, you always have good ideas; give me an idea,' he said. 'What should I buy her?'

I thought about it for a moment and then said I had an idea. He got out his pen and pad, his face full of anticipation as he prepared to write it down. I think he was expecting me to say that he should get an expensive ring from Tiffany, or a glitzy new frock, or something like that. But I didn't.

'Buy her a memory,' I said simply.

'What on earth do you mean?' he said, looking both aghast and slightly disappointed.

'Where is the best restaurant in town?' I asked.

He told me.

'Have you ever taken her there?' I asked.

'No,' he said.

'Why don't you book a table for the evening of her birthday and take her there?' I suggested. 'Better still, take the day off work, take her shopping and then go to the restaurant in the evening for a romantic meal.'

The next time I saw this fellow, he came straight up to me and threw his arms around me.

'Thank you so much,' he said, with a huge grin. 'My wife was utterly thrilled. We had a wonderful afternoon and evening

115

together. She said it was the best present I had ever got her and talks about it every day.'

Don't ever underestimate the power of giving someone a wonderful memory. We all have the opportunity to touch one another's lives every day and should use that privilege carefully.

I keep in constant touch with all my clients and send all of them birthday cards every year. I still remember one elderly client calling me up to thank me for remembering his birthday. When he told me that it was the only card he had received, it nearly broke my heart. But I knew that I had made a difference to his day. I had given him some pleasure and that meant a lot to both him and me. I hadn't sent the card as some sort of cynical ruse to get more of his business. I did it because I like to stay in touch with my clients and build a rapport. But, at the same time, when this fellow has to buy a financial services product, where do you think he is going to go?

It does not cost anything to give someone a pleasant memory. It really is as simple as treating people as you would like to be treated yourself.

One of my favourite ever stories is about a guy who gets into an elevator and turns to everyone and says hello and smiles. Of course, everyone just looks a bit nervous in return, unsure of how to react to this cheerful stranger. However, in a situation like this, most people will at least manage a curt nod and a half-smile in response, which they do. The next day, when this sociable chap climbs into the lift, he does the same thing. One of his fellow lift travellers sums up the courage to ask, 'Do I know you?'

'Yes,' replies the man brightly. 'We met yesterday.'

Remember, if you see someone in the street and smile, they will smile back. If you raise your fist to them, they will raise their fist to you. Which would you prefer?

Break the ice

Many people, whether or not they are in sales, have trouble talking to large crowds. Colleagues in the industry have often asked me how I manage to come across as so relaxed and happy at my seminars. They tell me that they are OK on a one-to-one basis with clients, but in front of a crowd they just dry up. Yet speaking in front of an audience is a useful skill that any salesperson would be prudent to learn because, as I have shown here, talking at large events can be extremely lucrative.

I always tell people that there are two tricks to talking to a large and small group. The first is to look for 'kind eyeballs' and the second is to treat it as though it is a one-on-one interview. Break the ice, relax and tell a few jokes and you will be fine.

When I am speaking at my seminars, I don't ever look at anyone in the audience in particular. I see everyone, but I see no one, rather like an actor on the stage.

Somewhere in that room is someone with really kind eyeballs, though. It is usually only one person, although on some occasions there may be two. What these kind eyes are saying is, 'I am listening to what you are saying and liking you.'

It does not matter if the other 99 people in the room are not fully engaged or willing to acknowledge that they are in tune with what you are saying. As long as you have got one person there with kind eyeballs you will be able to relax. Once you relax as a speaker, the rest is easy and before long everyone will be fully engaged.

Often at the end of my seminars I will go up to the person who has looked upon me kindly.

I will say, 'I see you have kind eyeballs. Thank you.'

They may not entirely know what I mean, but I am always grateful for their kind look because they will have helped me to relax.

I am lucky that I have a natural instinct to see, hear and observe things that others often miss. Often I don't even notice that I am doing it, but the information I log as I go about my business always seems to help break the ice.

I'll give you an example. When I saw some clients in Ipswich it came up early in the conversation that an important football match was being played that evening

I turned to the man I was seeing that day and said with a smile, 'You're brave.'

'Why is that?' he asked, looking bemused.

'Well, you are a Norwich City supporter, aren't you, and this is Ipswich,' I said.

'How did you know that?' he exclaimed.

'Ah, I noticed the Norwich City scarf hanging in your hallway cupboard when you hung my coat up,' I replied.

Straight away we had a rapport. He explained that he had moved from Norwich to Ipswich, so sometimes he had to keep his head down! We wouldn't have had that easy bond if I hadn't noticed the scarf when I walked in.

I have always found that top salespeople are gifted with an automatic power of observation. Over time they enhance that gift by training themselves to look out for signals and signs that may be of use later on. They notice things that most other people ignore. It is not done in an obvious fashion. They don't do it because they want to use it as part of their sales patter. They just clock it because it might be of use in establishing an easy rapport. It sets the relationship. People like to see that you are interested in them, or their background, or what they are doing. It breaks the ice and communicates.

Anyone can do this, though, even if they are not gifted with tremendous powers of observation. Sadly, too many salespeople don't like anything that smacks of 'training'. They think no one can tell them how to do something, or show them a better approach, because they know it all. Actually, they don't know it all. No one does. We can and should learn things every day. Even the greatest actors in the world are trained and continue to train throughout their career.

Humour is the greatest antidote

Not every day will go as planned. You may not get that job you wanted. Someone may let you down. Or that amazing sale you were absolutely sure would come through may not materialise. But there is always another chance. There is always a ray of sunshine on the horizon. All you have to do is look for it and keep your spirits up so when it does come along you are ready to grasp the opportunity with joy and alacrity.

I have found that there are moments of fun, happiness and stupidity every day. Even if they are not immediately obvious, I look for them, because they are always there.

Going back about 30 years ago, when I was working in America, I stopped for lunch at a McDonald's burger joint. As I was sitting there eating my burger and contemplating my next appointment, a chap who was obviously heavily disabled came in. I was appalled to see that the other people in the diner shied away from him and waved him away. Some people were even rude enough to tell him not to sit near them. My heart went out to this man and I motioned him over to sit next to me.

It turned out he was a really charming and nice person to talk to. He was in sales, just like me, and sold brushes for the American firm Kleeneze. We had a really interesting half an hour and were in stitches of laughter as we exchanged war stories from our life on the road. I can honestly say that I enjoyed my time with my new companion tremendously. Then, as I got up to leave for my appointment, he became serious for one moment.

As he shook my hand he looked into my eyes and said, 'Thank you very much for sharing your time with me, because these others wouldn't.'

I knew exactly what he meant, and what he said was important to me and touched me deeply. More importantly, though, I had got something very special out of meeting this chap too, which is why I remember that afternoon vividly to this day even though it happened so many years ago. I had spent a most pleasant and amusing period in his company and felt spiritually all the richer for the experience. That is, to me, what life is all about.

I do always say to myself, think nice things and welcome new experiences into your life. If there are sad things, don't let them weigh on you. If there are good experiences, let them lift you up. We all do have a choice in every situation that we find ourselves in. Life is, after all, what you make of it.

My life has not all been plain sailing. I have had moments which have floored me, but I have always used humour and joie de vivre to bounce back. When something upsets me, I think that I must learn from it and make sure that I don't ever put myself in that situation again.

Not every difficult situation is under your control. But there is no point cursing your bad luck, curling up in a corner filled with bitterness and giving up completely. When I was around 22 years old, I fell out with a client badly. He said I had done something to offend him, although to this day I still don't know what it was. He wouldn't give me an order that day and sent me away with some very harsh words. I sat outside this client's office in my car crying, because I was so hurt and upset. He even phoned my company to complain about me. For a brief while, I thought my world was about to come to an end. I really did.

Then I sat down and thought it through. I had no idea what I had done; indeed, I don't think I had actually done anything. Therefore, as I did not know what I was dealing with, I could only pick myself up, dust myself down and resolve to get everything 100% right for all my other clients. That was exactly what I did. I put a smile on my face and carried on.

Do you know what? Not only did I immediately feel better, but my clients could see I was relaxed and happy too. Then, within a couple of weeks, the person I had fallen out with returned to the company and carried on dealing with me as though nothing had happened. Ironically, it was through him that I later met my lovely wife Sherry.

You never know what is going to happen and what hand fate will deal you in the future. But, if you keep a smile on your face and maintain a cheery disposition, the possibilities are endless. Dealing with pain helps you move forward with your life. It helps you think and react in a different way. Once you start thinking, I won't let that drag me down, I won't let that destroy me, you will find the funny side. I guarantee it.

Far too many salespeople let small setbacks drag them down. I always say, find a way through it. If you have a problem at work or at home, the only way to deal with that problem is to deal with it. So go and deal with it. If you don't, it is like a cancer hanging over you, getting worse and worse, dragging you down and everyone around you.

In life, if you are lucky and work hard at it, you will end up doing what you want to do the most. Once you find your unique ability and work on it, you will have so much fun it is not true.

In many ways, the simple missive to 'have fun' is a summary of everything I have talked about throughout this book. If you believe in what you are doing, work hard and do your utmost to help your prospects trust you and feel at ease, you will succeed as a salesperson. Sure, there will be a few hiccups on the way and I can't guarantee every day will be a soar-away success, but if you stay positive, imagine the fun you could have while your sales career reaches new heights.

Having fun is the common thread which ties it all together. Becoming a successful salesperson is all about going out there every day, always believing and never giving in. It is about never allowing the market to dictate to you, but always dictating to the market. You need buckets of self-belief and, in my case, a belief in something beyond has made all the difference to me too. The important thing is to find whatever works for you and keep moving forward.

Some people make things happen. Some people watch them happen. Some people don't know anything happened at all. I have always preferred to be in the first group. What has happened in my life has happened because of me, not despite me. I made it happen that way. You could argue that I could have made it better, but no one can say I didn't make it work in the way I said it would.

Each day is a fun day. It is a bonus, because after all one day we won't be here. We will be somewhere else. I hope that somewhere else is an even better place, but I am still determined to enjoy everything while I am here. I am not prepared to settle for second best and you should never be either. This is the secret to success in life as well as sales.

So lift your head high, put your best foot forward and go out there and do it!

Good luck.

Acknowledgements

There are so many people whom I would like to acknowledge in this book who have helped me to achieve so many things, but in essence I would just like to thank all of those who have helped me along the way and taught me so many lessons. In particular, I think of Eric Oakman, Jim Wallinger and Tony Ward, who so many years ago put me on the right road. In more recent years I have been enormously indebted to the Million Dollar Round Table, an international organisation for top salesmen, where I have learnt so much sitting at the feet of 'masters'. Also deserving of credit are my strategic coach Dan Sullivan in Toronto, from whom I have learnt so much over the last 15 years, and my very good friend Ron Roge in New York. Ron, through his immortal line 'today, the markets will open and the markets will close', has taught me to be more relaxed when the markets panic.

Finally, I must acknowledge the help of my ghostwriter Teena Lyons, who has helped me enormously over the year it has taken me to put this book together.

About the Author

John T. Cross has 'been on the road' as a salesman for 50 years. He started as a trainee salesman at age 18, and although he has had various titles and worked for different companies along the way, he has only ever been a salesman. He has been a financial advisor for very nearly 40 years.

John T Cross has been happily married to his wife Sherry for 48 years, has two adult children and seven grandchildren ranging in ages from 7 months to 18 years. Away from work he has a strong interest in music and the theatre. He is something of a sports fanatic with a keen interest in soccer as a Tottenham Hotspur fan and Wembley season ticket holder.

As those that read this book will see, John has a very simplistic attitude towards what it takes to be a success in sales, and indeed life. He is in great demand as a public speaker and has spoken on every continent throughout the world.